CHILDREN IN CRISIS

SAGE HUMAN SERVICES GUIDES, VOLUME 12

SAGE HUMAN SERVICES GUIDES

a series of books edited by ARMAND LAUFFER and published in cooperation with the Continuing Education Program in the Human Services of the University of Michigan School of Social Work.

A **SAGE** HUMAN SERVICES GUIDE **12**

CHILDREN IN CRISIS
A Time for Caring, A Time for Change

Carmie Thrasher COCHRANE
David Voit MYERS

Published in cooperation with the Continuing Education Program in the Human Services of the University of Michigan School of Social Work

SAGE PUBLICATIONS
Beverly Hills / London / New Delhi

9.95
net

For information address:

SAGE PUBLICATIONS, INC.
275 South Beverly Drive
Beverly Hills, California 90212

SAGE PUBLICATIONS LTD
28 Banner Street
London EC1Y 8QE

Printed in the United States of America

Library of Congress Cataloging in Publication Data

Cochrane, Carmie Thrasher.
  Children in crisis.

  (Sage human services guides ; v. 12)
  Bibliography: p.
  1. Problem children.   2. Child psychology.
I. Myers, David Voit, joint author.   II. Title.
HQ773.C6   362.7   79-20132
ISBN 0-8039-1386-9

THIRD PRINTING, 1986

CONTENTS

ABOUT THIS BOOK

CHILDREN IN CRISIS is a practical guide for the child care worker, regardless of professional or academic background. As is the case with other *Sage Human Service Guides,* the techniques presented herein have been fully field tested. They work. But they may not be to every reader's liking. The authors clearly state their philosophical positions at the outset. They believe that a child who is acting out or otherwise behaving inappropriately is a child who is hurting or who has not learned appropriate responses to given social situations. They do not believe that children are or can be inherently morally bad. The techniques they present flow directly from this perspective. They leave no room for harshly punitive or revengeful behavior on the part of an attending adult.

Like other volumes in this series, the positions presented are those of the authors. Professor Armand Lauffer of the University of Michigan is Series Editor.

PRETEST QUESTIONNAIRE

Before we begin, we suggest you use the following questionnaire and its examples to see "where you are now" so that you may later be able to discern any changes in your beliefs and responses that may have occurred as the result of having worked through this book.

Please read each situation carefully and then record in the space provided your immediate verbal and/or physical response. That is, what would you say and what would you do?

(1) Carolyn enters the speech therapy clinic on Monday morning by slamming the door, pushing James aside, and grabbing another client's coathanger, exclaiming, "Get out of my way, you dope!" Your first response, as her therapist, would be _____

_____

_____

_____

_____

(2) Nelson, usually an active but cooperative, mildly retarded child, is this morning sitting restlessly at his work station, mumbling under his breath, and simply not engaging himself in the familiar tasks presented to him. You, as his supervisor, have gently indicated that he should begin his work. Now, you walk to his table and hand his materials to him. He then breaks these materials apart, throws them on the floor,

and glares at you as he says emphatically, "Leave me alone!" You
respond _____

_____

_____

_____

_____

(3) You enter the classroom to see erasers flying, overturned desks, two
children crying, and two others in a physical "free-for-all." You
respond _____

_____

_____

_____

(4) As they both tug on the puzzle game, Ted screams, "It's my turn!—
lego!" and Linda counters, "I'm not through yet—turn it loose!"
Jamie, an onlooker, goes to the rescue of Ted by striking Linda on the
arm. And you respond _____

_____

_____

_____

_____

(5) "Make him stop, Ms. Elliott, make him stop!" shrieks George as he
runs by you on the playground. Charles, in hot pursuit, yells again and
again, "George is a goofball, George is a gooney bird, George is a

goofball. . . ." You're the physical education instructor responsible for these children. You respond by _____

_____

_____

_____

_____

(6) Two girls, carrying trays of paper cups filled with fruit punch, round a corner and collide with other students running down the hall. Punch splashes, ice is flying, dresses are stained, and the carpet is a mess. You're the school counselor who happens to be walking around this corner when the collision occurs. You respond _____

_____

_____

_____

_____

(7) As part of your instructional unit on China, you bring your mother's prized set of Oriental dolls to class. After school is dismissed for the day and while you are preparing to leave, you lift the dolls to discover that each has been considerably damaged—a leg missing here, the tiny robe torn away there, and so on. You are simply furious. You respond by _____

_____

_____

_____

_____

(8) "Mama, read me a story," "Can I have a drink of water?" "Daddy, I'm not feeling so good." "Mama, where's my teddy!" "What time is it?" "Is tomorrow Wednesday?" "Mama, whatcha doing?" "Daddy, come in here with me!" "Daddy, I'm scared." This staccato stream of state-

ments besets you at your daughter's bedtime each night. You and your spouse are irritated at this "attention-getting," "manipulative" behavior. You respond by _____

_____

_____

_____

_____

(9) If you allow hypoglycemic Helen to have a 10:30 a.m. snack each day to alleviate her medical problem, the other chronically ill pediatric patients will want a "treat," too. Marilyn's mother, among others, is adamantly opposed to between meals snacks for her daughter. You are the charge nurse on the morning shift at this pediatric hospital and Marilyn's mother comes to you with this problem. You respond by

_____

_____

_____

_____

(10) You are in a staff meeting to discuss the appropriate punishment for a group of three children who have been determined to have been the ones who "rolled" (draped with toilet tissue) all the trees in front of the group home. You suggest that the appropriate punishment is ____

_____

_____

_____

_____

After finishing this exercise, read carefully through the book. Later, suggested answers and further exercises will be presented.

PREFACE, OR...
"HOW WE BECAME SO BOLD AS TO WRITE..."

Before we launch into telling you why we wrote this book, we first would like to develop a common definition of the topic of this book: "crisis." It takes a bit of explaining because the term seems to be used in a variety of ways, from economic and political to personal and interpersonal. For us, crisis is an interactional and situational event in which a child care worker (parent, teacher, therapist, counselor, and so on) is experiencing distress because the actions of one or more children in a group are so different from the expected and desired behavior as to prevent or to interrupt the ongoing, planned activity of the total group. Further, crisis is acute, requiring the attending adult to intervene immediately in order to respond to the needs of the child who is acting differently and also to the needs of the other children who are present.

Thus our definition of crisis is broad; it encompasses a multitude of intense emotional reactions in both the responsible adult and the identified client or child. Crisis emotions can range from simple, momentary frowns of disappointment, followed by withdrawal and pouting, to rage, followed by overt physical aggression between group members. Dynamically, "crisis" behaviors occur when a child has run out of, or has never learned, effective, rational, and purposeful behavior for the solution of interpersonal differences. Crisis behavior is relatively primitive, irrational, and ineffective. Being so, these behaviors have the potential for destructive, thwarting and damaging effects on all involved. Learning how to "handle" crises, then, is a most important and useful skill. We hope to accomplish this task through the following pages so that crises can become skill-building opportunities for learning more effective ways of solving problems.

While most of our suggestions and examples deal with the acting *out* child (e.g., fighting, cursing, stealing, lying), do not forget that there are other children who show pain in other ways—the sad, withdrawn, sullen, depressed, too-quiet child. We could invent a new term and call these children "acting-*in*" children! Such children are often undergoing equally intense emotional pain, but display this in less physically disruptive ways. The child who does not sleep well, who nods all day, who is not eating well, who seems to be enjoying less and less, who stays at the periphery of group activities, who wants to be alone most of the time, and who cries silently is just as crisis-prone as the child who acts *out*.

These are the children whose "silent screams" for help should not go unnoticed nor unresponded to by caring grown-ups in their world. These "acting-in" children are obviously more dependent on adult and peer attention for their self-esteem and are sometimes labeled as "babyish, silly, or demanding." Some of us behave as if, after a certain chronological age, people "should" need no more emotional nurturance. Contrary to a view that speaks of "spoiling" a child, we insist there is hardly such a thing as too much loving, too much attention, too much caring. As Dr. Carl Sipprelle of the University of South Dakota has said, "Human need is not met by further deprivation."

So with these children *give*, do not withhold affection on any misguided principle that some child "should be old enough" to get along without it. Only when a child's expressed needs are met will his demanding behaviors gradually subside. Attention-getting behaviors are often a move on the child's part to reassure himself that the adults in his world do care for him and that he can count on them as dependable helpers. A child truly must have this kind of security in order to function effectively and develop the necessary positive self-concept that *leads* to independent, self-reliant behavior that marks maturity and adulthood. Be sure, then, when reading this book, that although many examples and illustrations concern the acting-out child, we do not intend to convey the message that the quiet ones are less important children. Rather, the acting-in children are generally viewed more compassionately when (and if) they are noticed. Our experiences suggest that identification is the most important issue for these children obtaining help in resolving their crises. The matter of what to do with the acting-out child, again from our experiences, is a more complex issue and thus receives the major but not exclusive focus of the book.

When we both were involved in work as clinical psychologists at the Athens Unit, Georgia Retardation Center, it was our function to serve as crisis workers when residents in the academic classes acted in disruptive ways to the extent that there was more trouble at the moment than could be handled by the regular crisis teacher. In this process we were repeatedly impressed with the fact that the attitudes and actions of attending adults were often directly contributory to the initiation and escalation of crisis behaviors on the part of the residents. Therefore, it became imperative not only to assist in handling disruption once it was full-blown, but also to identify and to change "crisis-o-genic" behaviors and attitudes of the adult staff. In fact, we originally thought of subtitling this book "How an Adult Can Act Like a Grown-Up When a Child Is Acting Like a Child!"

Our efforts to change adults' attitudes and behavior during crisis took the initial form of actual modeling and oral contributions in staff meetings and planning conferences. These procedures were later discussed at length by the psychology staff. The crisis teacher at that time was Mr. (now Dr.) Andrew Weiner. Other psychologists at the Center were Ms. Alice McWhorter (now Dr. Alice McWhorter Libet) and Dr. John L. Shultz. Ms. Robyn McDonald, a social worker, was also involved in conversations related to this continuous effort to change attitudes and behaviors on the part of the staff toward the many crisis-prone residents of that facility. After much discussion, head-scratching, and quiet reflection, ideas about desirable adult attitudes and actions were collected into a mimeographed booklet. These booklets became well-known by staff at the Athens Center and by the university trainees from many disciplines. Later, the booklets were requested by staff of other child care agencies.

Our temerity in presenting yet another book that deals with "how to work with children" was spawned by the success of these methods when used in the setting described above and also in other teaching and treatment situations. This book, then, is the distillation of much academic study combined with thousands of trial-and-error transactions between each of us and many individual children. It is a presentation of those grown-up attitudes and actions that *work* in preventing and in resolving problem situations. They have been hammered out and tested in situations too numerous to mention. We believe these methods will be valuable to parents and foster parents, to group workers and group leaders, to school teachers and counselors, to psychologists and psychiatrists, and to child welfare workers in adoptions, foster care, protective services, and institutionalized living situations.

Before moving on, we would like to thank the many children, parents, teachers, and other clients whose responses to our efforts have molded our thinking and enhanced our effectiveness in our endeavor to improve the quality of their lives. They have been and continue to be our real teachers.

Finally, as a stylistic note, we have chosen not to use the awkward but sex-fair he/she pronomial form, but rather have alternated using "he" or "she" and their derivative forms throughout the book. This approach is not perfect, but allows us to write in ways to which we have become accustomed without being unnecessarily sexist.

Chapter 1

INTRODUCTION, OR . . .

"FIRST YOU THROW AWAY YOUR PADDLE . . ."

This book originates from three related concerns. First, the need for *all* adult helpers to be able to react to disturbed (or disturbing) children from a constructive, rather than a controlling, point of view. Some children's behavior is so disturbing that an adult's response can easily be far from constructive. This statement is true for both lay people and for professionals. Unfortunately, it is even true for those professionals whose everyday work includes working with children in crisis or those facing such situations.

Second, and most important, children need to learn verbal (that is, nonphysical) solutions to problems. Such socially acceptable problem-solving skills may be even more important than academic skills in a young person's present and future life adjustment. Such social skills may be a critical factor in whether or not the individual can become and stay employed, in whether he or she can live with a family or in a group living situation, and in whether the person can adjust happily to all relationships with other people. Therefore, the social skills that attending adults model and teach may constitute the most important learning that they can transmit to the young people in their care.

Third, the attitudes and behaviors presented in this book are based on a strongly shared conviction of ours that adult-child relationships can be happy "teacher-student," and/or "helper-helpee" relationships quite as easily, and much more beneficially than as "ruler-subject," "dictator-peon," and/or "enemy-enemy" interactions. The adult is more influential on children and on their present and future behavior when acting as an *advocate* than as an *adversary*.

These three related concerns are based on several important philosophical underpinnings or values. It is important that you understand and appreciate the following values that we are espousing with respect to the conflict prevention and conflict resolution methods being presented in the following chapters. First, we hold the firm conviction that

> *the values and human dignity of the individual child (as recognized by these methods) are far more important than the establishment of "order" and quiet by frightening children (or others) into submissive postures.*

We grant that physical controls are sometimes, but quite infrequently, necessary when a child is completely out of self-control, but you should remember that these methods originated in troubled situations at a point *after* traditional commands, threats, and, sometimes, physical coercion had *failed* to result in an orderly situation.

Second, we believe that

> *teaching socialization skills is as important as teaching art or arithmetic or nutrition.*

Otherwise, there might linger a mistaken view that "that sounds good [the conflict resolution methods, for example], but if I did *that*, how would we ever get anything [art, arithmetic, and so on] *done?*"

Further, we believe that

> *child care workers must be grown-up enough to have their self-esteem insured via their accomplishments and their affiliative needs met through appropriate adult-adult relations in their private lives so that they do not need ego supplies in the form of "winning" in conflict situations with their students, or in the form of imposing their will and power on younger, smaller, and less-experienced persons.*

Soul-searching questions that a grown-up must continually ask when dealing with young people are: "Whose needs are being met now: mine or the child's?" "Which of us feels better about ourselves now: me or the child?" "Which of us felt enhanced by what I just did: me or the child?" Basically, you, the adult, have to be convinced of the worth of each student and that student's feelings. You must be dedicated to honoring the essential uniqueness of each student, and, thus, to abstain from trying to remodel each of your young charges over into duplicates of yourself—a widespread, but unfortunate, form of "psychological cloning!"

Finally, proponents of *power* methods of child rearing versus advocates of *verbal negotiation* methods seem often to differ in their answers to one basic question: What is the basic moral nature of human beings? Power persuaders reflect their belief that people are *bad* and that all efforts must be extended toward somehow "getting the bad out" of the child. With this as a goal, *all* methods (from scolding to physically painful punishments) are justified. The alternative view, demonstrated in the crisis prevention and crisis intervention methods discussed in this book, is that

> *a child is not bad in a moral sense, but only socially unskilled, underskilled, and/or "misskilled."*

"Man" is not born with a fully operational array of the social skills necessary for ultimate survival within the family and community. Thus, such skills *must be taught* to children. Young persons need to be carefully and deliberately taught which of their behaviors are acceptable to others and which of their actions interfere with happy interactions with family and friends. In this teaching, it is important to remember the powerful effects of modeling (i.e., demonstrating through your actions the behaviors that you desire the child to display). Clearly, "do as I say and not as I do," is an ill-fated and foolish message to give to our children that generates the very problem we hope to avoid! Modeling is one of the most powerful forms of learning. Disturbed and disturbing children painfully remind us of our own inappropriate behavior daily by mirroring (often in a magnified way) our lack of social skills in dealing with them and with each other.

The differing values and beliefs of the "power" versus the "teaching" models can be seen in differing patterns of "punishment." We do not advocate "teaching" through punishment, particularly because punishment has been shown to merely halt the behavior then in progress rather than to teach new behaviors. By punishment we mean any of the following measures: exclusions of the child from further learning opportunities in the classroom after he has already calmed down; getting the child "out of your hair" by sending him away physically (that is, to inhouse suspension, to the disciplinary officer, and the like); and/or venting your frustrations on a child who has just demonstrated an inability to come up with an effective, socially acceptable behavior. An old, but apt, cliché comes to mind: "Don't hit a fellow when he's down!" In other words, don't put a child through more stress, isolation, and pain just at a time when he is showing that he hurts, that he needs comfort, that he needs reassurance about his acceptance and safety in the group, and that he needs a chance to demonstrate, with the adult's guidance, more appropriate behavior in that situation than he has just shown.

Often, in meeting with staff to discuss how a certain problem situation might be handled, we were in the position of asking other staff if they really wanted appropriate behavior from a child or if they wanted *revenge!* Consider the following: A residential counselor states, "Oh, Alex is a clever little fellow. If he knows that I won't send home when he misbehaves late in the afternoon, he'll be good all morning!" So? At least Alex is acting appropriately most of the day!

In other situations, the staff person may propose punishment in the form of writing a certain sentence many times after some inappropriate behavior. For example, if Linda throws an eraser and hits another child, both children are counseled. Linda apologizes, retrieves the eraser, and returns to the classroom work then in progress. To us, this would constitute an acceptable and sufficient resolution of the problem—for Linda to now be acting appropriately. To other adults, Linda must be made to "remember," to "pay back," by writing "I will not throw erasers" fifty times. This method is a display of the adult's wanting—not appropriate behavior—but *revenge.*

Most of the time, the difference between "reparation" and revenge can be discerned by determining whether or not the assigned or assumed activity *flows from* the infraction, accident, or disruption, or whether the assigned or assumed activity is artificially derived by the attending adult. For example, mopping up the floor after spilling water is reparation; writing "I will not spill water on the floor" five hundred times is revenge!

Yes, we are fully aware of the religious, ethical, and social implications of the notion of "man being socially inept rather than morally bad." Such a premise is threatening to more traditional conceptualizations of "good and evil." We are convinced, however, that the *self-directed ethical behaviors* of a young adult taught by adult models of the "social skills persuasion" will be at a minimum as non-harmful to others and as enhancing of the dignity of self and others as the *other-directed, blindly obedient behaviors* of a young adult taught by more traditional, "spare-the-rod-and-spoil-the-child" adults. And in addition, the former will be a more resourceful, more competent, and more self-confident young person!

With our *values* thus clearly stated, let us now present two sentences which contain the essence of the *attitudes toward children* that are proposed in this book:

> *A child exhibiting inappropriate or disruptive behavior is*
> *a child who is in some way hurting. Adults should display*
> **grown-up** attitudes *and* responses toward children *who*
> *are in such* pain.

Each word in the preceding sentences has been very carefully chosen.

Grown-up is our term for being self-controlled, reasonable, caring, helpful, and logical. We are most grown-up when we can remain objective and effective when others around us are out of control, are causing us some problem—thereby expressing their needs and their pain.

Attitudes refer to certain perspectives or ways of viewing things which then become natural antecedents to certain behaviors or certain emotional responses. In this book, we are suggesting a change in how we ordinarily view certain behaviors of the child. If we change how we view or interpret specific behaviors, we will change our emotional response to those behaviors. These changes will facilitate positive, constructive outcome when responding to children in pain.

Responses include all of these thoughts and feelings, and subsequent actions, that flow from a different and more grown-up way of viewing the problem.

Toward implies a parity between two persons, rather than a polarity and/or an inequality between the two parties. *Toward* also indicates a movement by the grown-up into the child's world as it is then being experienced by the child. Part of the condition of being grown-up is the responsibility to be the party in charge of dealing with any problems when difficulties arise between us and children.

Children is used rather than "persons" or "people" (as might have been chosen, because the same responses can be helpful to all) simply to emphasize again that in the relationship between children and adults, the responsibility to "treat" and to "manage" is the adult's role. Children, as the recipients of the adult's helping, are our primary concern. In Chapter 5, which notes the ways in which these attitudes and methods may be used with other populations, the generality of this book becomes more evident.

Pain signifies our belief that disruptive behavior always signals that the person displaying it is in trouble in some way, that the person is usually in a problem situation that he does not yet have the skills to solve readily and effectively, and so is experiencing a degree of psychological or emotional pain.

In essence, this small book describes some of the techniques that we have found to be effective in both preventing crisis behaviors from occurring and in dealing with such problems if they do occur. Specifically, we do recognize that regardless of everyone's best efforts, some problems will occur from time to time whenever any group of children has not yet learned better ways of negotiating through a problem to a mutually satisfactory solution. Thus crisis intervention is emphasized equally with crisis prevention.

This book shares a view of children with problems that helps us keep a perspective on the situation. This view enables us to model and teach more socially adaptive behaviors and to react with both common sense and sound theoretical rationale. The theoretical bases evolve from what we know of child development, social learning theory, and personality theory. In Chapter 6, references are given to guide the reader to further academic study. However, within this book, it is not our intention to involve our readers with extended theoretical discussions. We would rather leave that to those of you who wish to pursue it on your own. For now we will stay with the techniques that might help you deal with behaviors.

We will present two sets of techniques or skills. In Chapter 2 we discuss *prevention* skills. In Chapter 3 we present *intervention* skills. Case histories and examples follow, with other areas for application of these skills and technical references completing our presentation. A posttest for an assessment of your learning and a chance to give us some feedback in the form of a questionnaire are found at the end of the book.

In further explanation of the belief that verbal solutions must be found to difficult situations, a document entitled, *Our Civil Rights*, written by the creative arts classes at Cassady Elementary School, Des Moines, Iowa, is included here to present several of our explicit values from a different angle.

I have a right to be happy and to be treated
with compassion in this room:
    This means that no one will laugh at
    me or hurt my feelings.
I have a right to be myself in this room:
This means that no one will treat me unfairly
because I am
    Black or white,
    Fat or thin,
    Tall or short,
    Boy or girl.
I have a right to be safe in this room:
This means that no one will
    Hit me,
    Kick me,
    Push me,
    Pinch me,
    or hurt me.
I have a right to hear and be heard in this room:
This means that no one will
    Yell,
    Scream,
    Shout,
    Or make loud noises.
I have a right to learn about myself in
this room:
This means that I will be free to
    Express my feelings and opinions

*Without being interrupted or
punished.*

Now, we suggest that you review your responses as recorded on the
questionnaire of the pretest section. How do the values and views as
expressed in this chapter relate to your own answers to those problem situations? Ponder this as you continue your reading.

Chapter 2

CRISIS PREVENTION, OR . . .
"AN OUNCE OF . . ."

At the onset of our discussion of prevention of problems, let us deal first with our attitudes about certain observable, common, child care workers' behaviors toward children in pain that have *not* seemed to be effective and then some alternative, more effective, ways of behaving.

The first common problem we find among child care workers is what we and others call

> *the* is/does *fallacy, or telling children that they* are *so and so because they* do *so and so.*

A general example of this is telling children that they *are* ugly, nasty, naughty, shameful, and so on, when they *do* something that the child care worker does not like. Often without realizing it, we find ourselves labeling and rejecting the entire child, when what we are unhappy with is a particular behavior or set of behaviors that the child engages in. We say (or think to ourselves), "Joan, you're an ugly, nasty girl," giving us nothing positive about Joan with which to work. We communicate to Joan that we expect her to be nasty and ugly. It is most important that we think of, and communicate to, children in ways that specify their behaviors and not their "essences." An example: "Joan, I don't like it when you pick your nose; stop it right now!" is a much better message to Joan than telling her "you're a nasty girl" when you see her picking her nose.

The former statement is fairer for several reasons. First, it tells Joan that it is something she *does*—not something she *is*—that is inappropriate or disturbing. Because it is something she *does,* it is something she can change. It is also something that you can help her to change. You are much more likely to effect change in what a child does, than in what she is. So, talking about what a child does is something both she and you can use constructively for change.

Second, labeling the behavior (the "does") rather than the child (the "is") keeps the adult aware that one set of "bad" behavior does not necessarily make a bad girl. If we say Joan is nasty and ugly, then we tend to expect her to be that way in all situations. If we say Joan picks her nose when she is left alone, there is a lot of room for us to see the better aspects of Joan—some of her "good" behaviors. The message is quite simple: Don't tell a child that she *is* bad, unkind, a liar, or stupid! Tell her the things that she *does* that are inappropriate; you will be giving her a chance to change and yourself a chance to change your perceptions about her.

> *The second inappropriate adult behavior is sarcasm, or the use of superior intellectual tactics to belittle a child.*

An example: "Johnny, I really *like* you when you scratch my face!" Sometimes out of exasperation, sometimes out of misguided "fun," but most times out of a simmering dislike, we say sarcastic things to children. When the adult does this, he is always inappropriate. We are giving three messages to the child: Our tone of voice tells him that we are angry with him, our words tell him that we approve of him, and the combination of the two tells him that we do not care enough about him to send an intellectually honest message. Sarcasm, as such, is wasted on children because it is a sophisticated way of communicating. If you must be sarcastic, save it for adults. Children are confused enough without making matters worse by talking above them or by indirectly expressing anger and dissatisfaction to them in a way that will not help them.

> *A third ineffective way of responding to children is the use of unrealistic threats, or telling children that if they do so and so, you will do so and so.*

"Lacey, if you get out of your seat again, I'm going to make you stand up for a week!" Closely akin to sarcasm is the use of really impossible threats or scare tactics to try to control children who are misbehaving. Individuals who respond to children in this way are clearly demonstrating a misunderstanding of their responsibilities and a lack of respect for the child with whom they work. A specific example: Joan is picking her nose again. Her teacher is very tired of calling her down for this behavior. He says, "Joan, if you don't stop picking your nose, I'm going to chop your fingers off so you won't have anything left to pick with!" Does that ring a bell? Have you ever threatened a child like that? Well, you say, sure I have, but I was just kidding. Kidding? That's sarcasm, and we have already talked about why that is inappropriate. There are other important reasons for not using unrealistic threats. On the one hand, the child might believe you and become anxious, easily frightened, and might cower in your presence—as if you were a monster. On the other hand, a more sophisticated child—or a child who has been exposed to threats several times—might figure out that you can't or won't back up with action the threats you make! In the example above, Joan may well know that her teacher will not cut her fingers off—so she continues to pick her nose! In any case, the child either becomes unnecessarily frightened or does not believe the threat at all. Neither outcome is best for the child.

> *Scare tactics—or using frightening stimuli to force the child into submissive postures—is a fourth ineffective way of responding to a child.*

Scare tactics are another form of threats that are sometimes used out of desperation to try to bring disturbing children under control. For example: Mark is terrified of masks. Whenever he sees one, he starts to whimper and clings to the closest adult. In the absence of a mask, however, Mark tends to hit other children and occasionally will pull their hair. Mark's teacher has become "fed up" with his hitting and hair pulling, and now, whenever he hits another child, the teacher grabs a mask from under her desk and runs after Mark with it. The result? Mark stops hitting and pulling hair in the presence of his teacher.

The method is effective, make no mistake, but it is emotionally equivalent to being threatened with your life for letting a library book become overdue! It is a barbaric, traumatizing, unjustifiably harsh manner of dealing with a child's inappropriate behavior. There are many better ways to handle such problems as Mark's hitting and hair pulling that do much less damage to Mark in the process. So, the next time you think about scare tactics with a child, picture a loaded gun to your head during income tax time or a knife to your throat as you find an overdue book, and think about how barbaric these ideas are to you. Remember, scare tactics are for the Mafia, not for child care workers. If you only have scare tactics available to you to use in controlling a child, it may be time for you to obtain consultation from a supervisor, psychologist, or an educator who can recommend some helpful ways of intervening with the problem behaviors of the child.

Now, enough of all the ineffective methods of dealing with children. Let us begin now to consider attitudes and methods that *do* work!

Of all the principles to remember that lead to a "grown-up" response to a child who is disruptive and angry,

the cardinal rule is to view anger as fear.

The angry child is only reacting to fear of loss. It may be loss of self-esteem, loss of her possessions, loss of her status within the group, and/or loss of her sense of being treated fairly. When the child's rights are threatened, she may defend against this in the only way she knows or has *seen* demonstrated by powerful adults: physical retaliation. Let us talk about this now from the general perspective of the responsible adult.

As an adult assesses the situation, there are a series of three questions he can ask himself—questions that will assist him in remaining objective, in assessing the situation accurately, and in responding appropriately to the angry child's needs. The first is:

What do I feel just now?

When the adult monitors his own feelings in this way, he may decide that if he feels preoccupied, the child is probably seeking attention. If the adult senses that he himself is angry, the child is probably seeking power. If the adult himself is feeling threatened, the child is probably seeking revenge. If the adult is feeling weak or hurt, the child is probably seeking some major control over the situation. This may also be conceptualized as the adult being "manipulated" by the child and the child's behavior. We have not found it to be particularly helpful in dealing with children to think of being manipulated by the child because this word implies an adversary relationship between the child and the adult and simply does not lead to a very effective interpretation of what is happening in the relationship. In addition, if the adult's role is that of caring for the child, it is his *responsibility* to respond to the child's expressed needs, no matter in what form those needs are expressed!

The second silent question the adult should ask himself is:

What does this child want?

The answer will probably be: "He wants to feel safe," "He wants to be important," "He wants to be treated fairly," "He wants to get attention from me," and the like. Then, the adult can empathize more completely with the child by following up with the third question himself:

Is it bad (crazy, unusual, unhealthy, unlike me, and so on) for the child to want this (to feel safe, important, and the like)?

The answer to this third question will invariably be "no!"

These think steps keep us as adults from misunderstanding a child, and more importantly, from impuning moralistic origins to his behaviors. "He's just bad" will never be our attitude or conclusion if we will ask ourselves the above three questions. In addition, by asking these questions of ourselves we reduce the risk of attributing sophisticated, cunning adult motives to the child's misbehavior—such as, "He's doing that *just* to make me angry," or "She really gets her kicks by being sweet to me one day and hateful the next." By paying attention to the three think steps, we can focus on determining what the child wants and needs, and then, begin work on teaching them how to fulfill these wants and needs more effectively and in more socially acceptable ways.

In using these think steps, the adult also can remind himself that there is a great difference between what a child *knows* intellectually, or can recite by rote about rules and procedures, and what a child *does* when he is under stress and in pain. For example, when a child is threatened, aroused emotionally, and/or afraid, he reverts to more primitive and less rationally based behaviors. Therefore, it is completely ineffective to "punish" a child for an infraction of a rule that occurs when he is strongly emotionally aroused. Also, because of this, the rational directives given by the adult have little chance of being heard, complied with, or even remembered while the child is upset. Therefore, the starting point is to let the child cool down and come to feel safe again. It is the adult's responsibility to teach self-control, problem-solving, and rational ways of acting. The adult does this by modeling such grown-up responses in times of crisis. When and if the adult in charge reacts in other than grown-up ways, the child does not have the chance to learn other behaviors that are more grown-up or more mature.

A problem situation *always* has origins and antecedents which lead up to outright physical aggression. Remember physical aggression is a modeled display of pain and an attempt to protect against personal loss of some kind. There are always reasons for "acting out" behavior. Although dealing with those behaviors is the subject of chapter 3, "Crisis Intervention Strategies," it is important that these principles be stated in our discussion of ways to *prevent* crisis. When there is a problem the only helpful consultant is a person who has created *prior, positive* relationships with the party or parties in conflict. This brings us to the central premise of this chapter:

> **Crisis can be prevented by the creation of positive relationships between children and adults.**

Recent research findings show dramatically that when a child is behaving in appropriate manners and *receiving sufficient recognition* for this behavior, the number of disruptive or inappropriate behaviors of that child decreases rapidly into nonexistence!

Further, it is the attending adult's responsibility to build a positive relationship with the child or the children in his care. Positive relationships can be built in the following ways.

1. BE A HELPER

Build an image of being a helper to the children rather than being a warden, a police officer, a judge, a threatening authority, or a power person. This image of being a helper can be reflected in a number of ways.

Comment to the child on everything he or she does that is adaptive, helpful, and appropriate. This builds the child's self-esteem and his confidence in his own abilities to control emotions and to express caring toward others. Examples are "John, that was really fine when you helped Mathew with his tray," and "Luke, you handled it well by walking away when Martha yelled at you."

Initiate positive, personalized interactions with children as "basic trust" builders. For example, instead of "Hi, Mark, how're ya doin'?", something like "Hi, Mark, you look kind of sleepy this morning," is a more personalized notice of something special and unique about him.

Follow through on any commitments made to a child. Only when others honor agreements made with him can he learn to honor his own commitments. We all too often think that children will not "remember" our commitments to them, only to find that they remember them better than we do. With children who have had many disappointments in life, we do them a disservice in taking our verbalized intentions regarding them as anything other than firm promises.

Grant in fantasy what it is impossible to grant in reality. For example, the child may say, "I want to go to the beach!" The adult might answer, "Wow! That sun and sand would be fun, wouldn't it? I wish we could go, too." (Not, "Well, that's just too bad, you know you can't go to the beach!") The former response is one of empathy with the child; the latter is one of an oppositional, "put-down" quality, turning the interaction into one of possible conflict.

Deal with problem events rather than attributing negative emotions or negative intentions toward the child. An example: The adult says, "Hey, the juice is spilled on the floor, what can we do to take care of it?" (Not, "Well, you've done it again; you just do that to bug me!")

Realize that a child's noncompliance to a directive from an adult can mean nonunderstanding of a directive, or can mean that the child has to deal with something else emotionally at that time; rather than that he is being willful and personally defiant toward the adult's position, power, or personality. In brief, a child's compliance or noncompliance often has little to do with the adult as a person. Keeping this in mind will help us remain objective about the incident and will keep us ready to provide additional information about what we want from the child, rather than responding to his noncompliance punitively out of feelings of having been personally rejected, defied, or challenged by the child.

Keep the child informed about our own feelings that relate to him and to his behavior. It is usually better to phrase such feedback in a statement beginning with "I feel . . ." rather than "You are . . ." An example would be the adult saying, "I feel frustrated when you throw the crayons on the floor. I need your help." (Not, "You are really being completely impossible today by throwing those crayons!") One very important caution: It is unfair and unethical for the adult, out of his own personal concerns, to use such feeling statements to make the children feel guilty, such as is contained in the statement, "I'm really sick today, and if you're not good, I'll have to go to the hospital." A supplemental stipulation in regard to sharing one's feelings with children is to be sure to share happy, pleased, loving, joyful, and appreciative feelings more often than negative ones.

This procedure about sharing feelings in words is also very important in teaching appropriate social behaviors to children. Two reasons for this: First, it teaches that it is O.K. to *have* feelings (both negative and positive ones). And second, it teaches the names of feelings, which will gradually enlarge the child's vocabulary of feeling words and thus enhance his ability to use these words and terms in problematic interactions with others, rather than having to resort to acting out the unnamed feelings in physical ways.

2. RESIST THE INCLINATION TO INDULGE THE CHILD IN HIS NEGATIVE BEHAVIORS

We forthrightly reject the idea that positive adult-child relationships can be built by adult indulgence of the child. An example of this indulgence would be to let the child have his own way—let the child do anything he wants. Such carte blanche permissiveness is absolutely terrifying to a child (as well as to us adults!) for he must then deal with the enormous problems of (1) where he begins and ends in relationship to his extraordinarily, overwhelmingly destructive powers; and (2) what is and is not, fatal to him. Adult indulgence can take another form: that of giving the child material gifts. This, too, may be well intended but it is also misguided. It teaches the child that the *adult* is the source of the child's satisfactions, that the *adult's* favor must be won in order for the child to receive the things he desires, rather than the adult serving as a guide to the child as he learns to satisfy his own needs through his own efforts!

Adult indulgence may also take the form of quite systematic issuance of bribes and threats regarding the child's future behavior. Most of the time, this is ineffective because (1) a younger child's sense of time is not so well-developed as to be able to deal with concepts of future; and (2) the child is thereby not given any credit for taking a rational perspective as opposed to working for tangible reinforcers. This system also translates into strong implications that a child is not likely to demonstrate altruistic motivation (without the prospect of material rewards). Further, if the child is ruled through fear (fear of losing anticipated rewards), the adult will never know when to stop threatening such loss, but instead will have to continue in this self-appointed role of "police officer" indefinitely.

This is not to say that token economies, tangible rewards, and the like are always inappropriate. Indeed, they are often necessary first steps in bringing children into contact with a potentially reinforcing natural environment. They are, however, only first steps and should not be perceived as ends in themselves. After certain behaviors are brought under control through simple contingencies (that is, receiving tangible rewards for appropriate behaviors), the task then becomes one of fading the strict, arbitrary contingencies into a naturalistic relationship with the environment. This simply means that we must then teach children self-regulated methods and strategies for cooperation, sharing, and empathizing with others so that these skills become the means for obtaining those things from the environment that are satisfying to them: recognition, status, freedom from fear, and the like. The direction of the learning process should always flow from arbitrarily chosen tangible rewards to the naturally occurring satisfactions. As a child's self-monitoring, self-control, and self-regulation of his own behavior become natural and habitual (through guided practice), significant others in his environment will act in response to his behaviors in ways that are satisfying to the child.

3. ELIMINATE THE THREAT OF PHYSICAL PUNISHMENT FROM YOUR REPERTOIRE OF INTERVENTION TECHNIQUES

Direct physical punishment, it has been learned through many, many learning experiments, only *stops the behavior then in progress.* It never teaches more adaptive, more appropriate, and desirable behaviors. It is incumbent on us then to employ proven procedures (mentioned and referenced in chapter 4) that include pro-social, effective ways of obtaining goals rather than simply punishing inappropriate behaviors without teaching alternative behaviors.

In summary, then, the most effective means of preventing a child from displaying disruptive, crisis-level behavior, is to have built a prior, positive relationship with that child—a relationship in which the adults' behavior model the behavior desired from the child; a relationship in which the adult is careful not to use domination of the child to meet his own needs; a relationship that permits, encourages, and guides the *verbal* expression of feelings, a relationship that teaches effective behaviors rather than focusing on punishing ineffective behaviors.

Chapter 3

CRISIS INTERVENTION, OR . . .
"THE POUND OF . . ."

Before getting into the one, two, three steps of what to *do* in a crisis situation, the responsible adult's attitudes and psychological posture should be examined. When hearing repeatedly about the rights of children, child care workers often raise the question of their own rights. An adult who attends children *does* have personal rights— the right to be treated in a certain way, the right to respect, and the like. But, these rights do not originate in the power of any position nor in the fortuitous circumstance of simply being bigger, older, or stronger than the child. Rather, the adult's rights originate from the same conditions as those of the child: the circumstance of simply *being human*!

The adult should recognize that she *is* only human (a fact that does not give her a right to behave in less than grown-up ways, but does give her, as an adult, the right to have feelings and to recognize that at times, she should call on another more objective grown-up to take over in a problem situation). For example, can she be calm enough herself to deal with a highly emotional situation? The adult should ask herself one quick question: "Am I objective enough to accept the fact that the outcome of this problem/situation may be that I myself precipitated the whole mess?" If the adult cannot accept a positive answer to this hypothetical question, it may indicate that a consultant or a colleague should be called in to direct the problem resolution.

Also, when an adult feels particularly negative toward a certain child, when the adult is afraid that she might lose control in dealing with the child, when the adult is short on patience and energy because of other drains on these resources—these are times when she should also call in another grown-up for assistance.

Another index to a person's capabilities in any given crisis situation is the volume of the voice used in speaking. A loud, tense, or strident voice reflects the intensity of a situation that is already emotionally overloaded.

Before getting into specific behaviors of the adult, it is also necessary to be clear about the purpose and meaning of various time-out procedures. The time-out booth (chair, or room) is not meant to be a prison cell used for punishment. It should be used for children who need a temporary cutback of environmental stimuli; children who cannot handle any more of the group activity at the moment; children who are becoming overloaded when trying to cope with a too-rich or too emotionally arousing environment at that time; and children who are just needing some quieter place and some additional time to deal with their own concerns and private thoughts. There has been a great deal of confusion in educational and psychological circles regarding the uses and effectiveness of time-out as a means for reducing undesirable behavior in disturbed or disturbing individuals. Recent research, however, has clearly shown that in order to have any effect on helping a child change his or her behavior, it is first necessary that the environment from which the child is removed is perceived by the child as positive, rewarding (i.e., a place the child would *like* to stay). Unfortunately, this is not true of many living or learning environments for many children. Thus, we suggest that time-out be used for a short-term (five-minute) respite for an emotionally overloaded child rather than for punishment.

Another important attitude that should be demonstrated by the adult is that of a willingness to accept *verbal* expression of negative feelings (such as cursing, name-calling, and the like) as undesirable but as highly preferable to physical aggression. If such name-calling or cursing is upsetting other children, deal with both children and work out some agreements about this kind of behavior. But the goal of behavioral guidance is always to teach the child to interact with others, particularly in problematic situations, on a verbal rather than physical plane.

Finally, remember above all that the child's maladaptive behaviors may stop momentarily if she is physically or verbally punished but such punishment leads to no new learning of more adaptive behaviors. A child does not learn nor grow nor develop nor adapt in an atmosphere of fear. But rather, only when she feels safe and relaxed in an atmosphere of being lovingly guided do more adaptive behaviors evolve. In addition, this final attitude works to the benefit of the attending adult as well: It simply feels better to be *loving* than to be engaged in power struggles.

Now, suppose that even in the best of all possible worlds and with the best of all possible attitudes and feelings toward the children involved, the situation still literally explodes! The explosion reflects an intensity and a power from the involved parties that not only cannot be ignored, but that also carries the real possibility of physical hurt coming to one or all of the children in the situation.

The steps involved in intervening in this crisis situation include controlling the situation, listening fully, exploring alternatives, agreeing on present and future behavior, and resuming normal activities. From the initial letters of each of these steps, we suggest the mnemonic device, CLEAR. Now let us examine in detail each of the steps in turn.

1. CONTROL THE SITUATION

This control consists of effecting immediate separation and/or isolation of the parties involved. For example, if two children are in the process of physically debating a point, it serves no useful purpose to allow them to keep on swinging or screaming at each other. Separating the children is like separating the fuel from the fire. In general, the more noise the child is making, the lower the voice of you, the adult, should be. If this does not seem possible, it will be extraordinarily difficult to "establish a beachhead," as our colleague, Dr. David R. Parker, calls it. A low voice, but with "command" quality (a cool firmness) is necessary. As soon as you step in, you must immediately "travel" (emotionally and intellectually) to the child's frame of reference. As you are reacting physically, you must also be mentally assessing the factors that might have precipitated or contributed to or maintained this crisis as related to that child's subcultural values and indigenously appropriate behaviors (e.g., the rules of how conflicts are handled in her neighborhood, family of origin, or previous school).

What we are assuming here is that you have some idea about what these values might be and how they affect behavior. If not, you have some further work to do in addition to resolving the present conflict: finding out what the values are and how they interface with the values of other members of the group in which the conflict arises. Just as it was important that you understand *our* values underlying how we think conflicts should be resolved, it is no less important that you understand the values operating within the individual members and the group as a whole with respect to what values they hold about how to resolve conflicts. Remembrance of, and use of, the three think steps in assessing a problem situation are effective here. "What do I feel just now?" "What is the child wanting now?" and "Is it bad for her to want that?"

When handling a crisis situation in a group, never back a child into a corner where she has no other alternative but to strike back physically. If she "loses face" before her peers, so do you in the long run. Try always to give her "face-saving" options for her choice of responses.

There are occasions in which physical restraint of the child is imperative to avoid serious physical harm from coming to one of the persons in the situation. There are training courses that teach appropriate use of physical intervention techniques for use in restraint of physically aggressive clients. These courses are not only valuable in teaching competencies in these techniques, but are also useful in giving you a different "set," or attitude, toward aggressive clients. We have found that when an adult does come to feel capable of handling even quite turbulent physical situations without harm to self or to client, that adult comes to have a different and more self-confident posture and poise, so that there is actually a decreased likelihood of ever having to use physical intervention techniques! That is, these trained adults use force only when it is really required and not just to reduce their own distress about things getting out of control.

In general, however, physical restraint should be used only as a last resort. To physically conquer a child only reinforces what she already knows, that you are bigger and stronger than she is and that "might makes right!" Thus, all teaching about *verbal* methods of conflict resolution stops at that time because you are demonstrating to the child that force is the way that conflicts are handled—just what we do *not* want her to learn! Power struggles that involve extreme physical force are momentary victories for whichever party happens to win. They clearly show that you, the adult, have run out of logical, rational, and grown-up responses.

One of the times when physical restraint becomes necessary is when the child in pain is acting out and doing so to the extent that her actions may cause real harm to herself or others. When a child is completely out of (her own personal) control, it is then a form of caring to exert external control. These restraints should be the lightest touch sufficient to detain the child from further destructive behaviors. She should be held and told over and over, "When you are calm, I will turn you loose," "When you can be in control again, I will let go," and the like. The grown-up should not extend such physical control a moment beyond when it is actually needed. Gradually reducing the force you are applying to restrain the child, while telling her what you are doing, is a good way to test if the child is ready to resume responsibility for her own behavior.

When attempting to resolve a crisis, it is important that there be no audience, especially peers who have a tendency to reinforce maladaptive behaviors. Many, if not most, children get a charge out of seeing emotional displays. More about this later.

The primary goal in a crisis is to handle *that* crisis and not to dig up all the past sins of the child. Further, the goal is not to attempt to buy insurance against all future problems. The adult is often feeding her own ego (that is, satisfying her own personal needs) if she gives the child long lectures, threats about what will happen if such occurs again, and the like. Further, if a child learns, by watching an adult behave in such a child-like manner, that certain behavors of hers can precipitate circus-like fireworks from the adult, she will tend to repeat those maladaptive behaviors. Children like excitement, explosions, high drama, big reactions from adults. If they can reliably trigger such explosions from adults, they often will—just to see the show! It should be remembered, however, that big reactions can just as easily and much more effectively be positive, as when a "big deal" is made to celebrate the occurrence of happy or positive events and achievements.

2. LISTEN FULLY

Once you have separated the feuding parties, it is time to find out the facts and the feelings of the children involved. What happened? When? What part of what agreement was believed or perceived differently by the children involved? In brief, what happened to lead to this situation?

Never ask a child *why* she did something. You will either get hostility, fear, or a lie as a response. Most often, children are unaware of *why* they did or felt something. This is because most feelings are multiply determined; most behavior is the result of many factors. If the child truly does know, her only answer has to be "I didn't know a better way," or in other words, "Because I'm stupid!" The companion, but equally ineffective question is "Why didn't you . . .?" This leads the child to the same inevitable answer, insofar as she is aware, "Because I'm stupid!" However, if asked what happened, or where, or when, the child can answer you without being backed into a humiliating psychological corner. The child can tell you what happened (at least from her point of view), if you ask, and if you truly listen to her story with caring and with patience.

There is a particularly effective manner of listening. It is derived from and similar to the listening skills labeled "Active Listening" by Thomas Gordon in his work, *Parent Effectiveness Training*, and as "Reflective Listening" by Virginia Satir in her discussions of communications skills. In essence, the carefully listening adult responds to the upset child's statements by reflecting, noting, and labeling the "feeling states" demonstrated by the child rather than to the words said by the child. For example, if a child said, "He told me he was going to give me an airplane and he didn't do it!" the adult, instead of responding, "You didn't get the airplane you wanted," would more sympathetically and empathetically respond, "You were disappointed," or, "You feel *disappointed* because you didn't get the airplane like he told you." You can always know that your reflective response has been accurate about the child's feeling state if, in reply, the child says, "Yeh." This "yeh" is emitted by the child along with a sign of relieved recognition and appreciation of having been understood (e.g., fists are dropped, frowns are lifted a bit, posture is shifted to a less tense or rigid one).

Recognize at the onset that the "facts" as stated may or may not be true. Don't worry about the accuracy of such facts. Be more concerned about how the events *as remembered by the child* could have led to her pain.

Focus on the immediate problem at hand, which is the child, not the rules and regulations of the situation, the classroom, the institution. At that moment, really listen, attempting simultaneously to see and even to experience the world as the child apparently is experiencing it at that time. Stay with the child, both physically and emotionally. Use loving physical gestures such as a hand on her shoulder or on her arm as well as verbal responses to provide support to this child who is in pain. Let the child know that you care.

A word of caution, however, is in order about physical assurances. Such touching is really a dynamite maneuver. It can be extraordinarily helpful, or, if misinterpreted or offered at the wrong time, it can be very detrimental to the situation at hand and to the general relationship between the child and you. The way that you know that touching can be accepted by the child at that time is by watching the child's body language. For example, if she is standing with arms outstretched in front of her and elbows locked, she is holding you away. If she is standing with her own arms across her body, she has erected a barrier against you or anyone else intruding on her physical and psychological space. If you move toward her physically and the child takes a few steps back away from you or turns her head away, stop; do not go any nearer the child at that time. Another alternative is to *ask* a child at some point, if you are not sure about her accessibility. For example, give a proximity invitation to a chair beside you, saying "There's a chair here if you'd like to sit down," or you can ask the child, "Is it O.K. if I come over there to talk?"

Always give a child a chance to tell her side of the story completely, unhurriedly and fully. Do not allow anyone in the situation to interrupt the child while she is talking. Be careful yourself, as the adult, not to interrupt the child while she is telling her part of the story. In allowing the child to tell you what happened, you have already elicited from her a verbal response rather than a physical one, which is exactly the direction in which all crisis intervention work should move.

It is very important that you allow the child a chance to tell the story, even if you were physically present when the altercation

took place. You must never assume that you know what happened.
You *do not know* what was interpreted or experienced by that upset
child. It is very important that the child knows that she has the
right to fully express her own point of view about what just happened and her own feelings about that set of circumstances. Many
adults in this situation become concerned that a child will lie or
distort the truth. Our experience suggests that this happens much
less often when a child has the knowledge that she will be heard
clearly and completely about her perceptions regarding what happened. Thus, the child will not need to exaggerate or distort the
events beyond that which naturally occurs in emotionally laden
situations in order to get your attention and consideration.

Always let the child in pain know that you personally care about
what she is going through and that you are aware of her hurt and
upset. Own your own messages during this time. That is, take responsibility for your own responses and be sure that they are objective, concerned, firm, and loving. Such pat phrases as "It's all over
now," "Everything's going to be all right," "I know just how you
feel," and the like are *not* helpful. The child will recognize them
as the pat, stock clichés that they really are and so will not feel
personally comforted by them. The fact of the matter is, you do not
know that things are going to be better or that you know just how
someone else feels or that it is really all over for them now. By
making such well-intentioned but inaccurate statements to a child,
you actually communicate how *little* you really understand.

If you wish to communicate such reassurances, you first have
to actively listen, as mentioned earlier, and then reflect statements
that contain specific feelings and content that you have heard from
the distressed child. An example of a more realistic reassurance
might be: "You seemed really frightened when Luke swung the
baseball bat at John (child nods affirmatively). O.K. Now did you
just hear Luke say that he would tell John when he is angry at him
next time and not use the bat? (Answer 'yes.') O.K. then, how do
you feel now?" This approach is more time consuming, for sure,
but generates real confidence in children in their own *and* your
perceptions and reassurances.

Keep in mind that your immediate goal is to de-escalate this
crisis situation regardless of what it is about. It does no good to
try and make complicated verbal points, to teach values, or even

to do much talking at all while the child is still "sky-high." The child is just not with you at that time, anyway, and further, she is sure to resent your use of logic when she is in an emotional state. She is just not in touch with your logical stance at the moment. She is not even much in touch with her own feelings at that moment.

As the crisis de-escalates, demonstrate empathy, warmth, extreme interest, and undivided attention, but be very firm in your messages. Let the child know that her behavior cannot continue, that a solution will be worked out, and that she must participate in this problem-solving activity. When the child has calmed down somewhat and is capable of understanding and reporting what happened, be sympathetic but send a definite message regarding your own feelings about the situation. Be sure this message comes from someone who sincerely cares. An example at this point might be an adult who says, "This situation is just too much. We cannot go on until we get this worked out." Such a statement does not blame any one participant. It simply and forthrightly states that things are in a mess and strongly implies that such may not continue. When the crisis situation is sufficiently de-escalated and the child is capable of some thinking, bring all of the parties, including any staff or family involved, together and get a report from each person in turn as discussed above. Allow no one to interrupt another person. When parts of the puzzle are reconstructed in this manner, restate your own understanding of what happened and of the origins of that situation that led to the feelings as expressed by each of the participants.

3. EXPLORE ALTERNATIVES

First, instruct all participants about what is going to happen next. Restate the problem in terms of your understanding of what happened and of what each person wants. Inform the participants that now, each of them can suggest ways in which each of them can respond differently. It is most important, however, that while such solutions are being suggested, no one may interrupt while another person is speaking. Further, no one may criticize or reject any solution until all such plans are listed. And after all such solutions are listed, each person may then state their willingness to

accept or to reject each solution in turn as each is discussed. This
process will continue until a solution is found which is acceptable
to all parties involved. (And you, the adult, are usually one of the
parties involved!) Then begin this process by inviting each participant—one at a time—to suggest solutions. The generation of
alternatives may be a fluid, freely flowing exchange, or the parties
may be silent and unresourceful. In the latter case, you may need
to supply several alternatives for review and evaluation by the
participant.

Allow each individual to reject any given alternative, and do
not press that person for reasons why the alternative is unacceptable
to her; rather simply discard that alternative. Continue, with each
participant in turn, until only acceptable alternatives remain on
the list, or until (as sometimes happens), no alternative remains.
In the latter case, it now becomes the job of all involved to generate
new alternatives and to redo the evaluation process. It is usually
more effective to adopt "the rule of brainstorming": to allow no
one to criticize an alternative as it is being submitted. It is often quite
helpful to write down each alternative as it is suggested; then, as
the generation of alternatives seems to slow or to stop, to go back
through the list, citing each alternative and asking "Mark, is that
all right with you?" then, "Mary, is that acceptable to you," and
so on.

Keep working with the parties involved until an alternative is
agreeable to all parties. This can take a long time, but remember,
socialization is a life-long process! When the process seems inter-
minable, it is most likely due to you having too quickly cycled
through step number 2, listening. If everybody involved is com-
fortable that they have been heard and understood by you, it is
likely that they will have also heard and, to some degree, understood each other as well. If this understanding of each other has
not occurred to some extent, unanimous agreement on any one
solution will be unlikely. So, if you get bogged down at this point,
finding one or more alternatives acceptable to those involved,
it's time to focus directly on making sure that everyone understands
each others' position. This may sound difficult, but it usually only
requires that each person state the other's position until he ob-
tains agreement from, say, John that, yes, that is his position. Then
proceed to Mary and so on until everybody has stated everyone

else's position about what happened. It is important to note, however, that children sometimes confuse stating someone else's position with endorsing it! Making this distinction for them surely sim-
plifies this intermediate step. At this point you will very likely have
some acceptable alternatives to work with.

4. AGREEMENT ON THE SOLUTION

If two or more alternatives are acceptable to all concerned, then
pick the simplest! When a solution is agreed on, have all parties
voice their understanding of the solution and what their own role
will be in implementing that solution. Nail down exactly who is
to do what, when, where, and how! In our experience, more agreements have broken down because the participants were unclear
about these details then because of intentional disregard of previously made agreements. Having everybody recite what they are
going to do, specifically, will save many headaches and "broken
promises."

It should be noted that consequences for the participants if they
do not do what has been agreed on are not projected at this point,
and such actually never come into play. That is, a threat or a penalty
to one of the participants for "not keeping her word" or "not doing
what she said she would do" is never specified. To do so would be
the construction, not of a positive solution, but of a system of rewards and revenge. As a part of the working through to a positive
solution to whatever problem has surfaced or led to the crisis, it
is important that both (or all) parties involved can "confess" (apolo-
gize) and make any reparation (amends) possible at this time. This
confession and reparation procedure follows from William Glasser's
work, known as "Reality Therapy."

Making appropriate (that is, situation-specific) positive responses, referred to above, after a crisis is a learning experience
for the child. Such learning experiences are the kind and content
of "discipline" as proposed here. Such discipline shows the child
that the attending adult cares enough to get to the bottom of the
problem, to hear her out fully, and to help her to act in constructively appropriate ways from that time on. This is "discipline" de-
fined as helping and teaching, not as punishment, as we discussed
in chapter 1.

5. RESUMPTION OF REGULAR ACTIVITIES *OR* RENEGOTIATION BACK THROUGH CLEAR STEPS TO ANOTHER SOLUTION

After the crisis is over, when a new solution to the situation has been agreed on by all participants, the children are then reinvolved in appropriate activities and the crisis participants turn their energies toward demonstrating appropriate behaviors in the situation. This reinvolvement ends the encounter on a positive note. Let the child or children walk out of the crisis resolution encounter with the knowledge that you, as an adult, have respectful, positive feelings about her or them even if you have just deplored and redirected her or their previously inappropriate behavior. Reassure the children of your continuing desire to be helpful in learning new behaviors.

If after de-escalating the situation you suspect that the children, still have even mild anxiety about the situation, don't let them leave your presence. Stay with the children until it is clear that they are really calm, "together," and again in control. Think of this as "putting out a fire" and being sure that there are no lingering "sparks" that, if left unnoticed, can quickly lead to fire again. After handling the immediate crisis situation, try to prevent this from becoming contagious. If appropriate, go back to the place of the crisis and get everyone involved "squared away" and involved in the next appropriate activity. Again, be sure *never* to tell a child to stop doing something without also telling her what *to do*. "Now, Mary, you stop that right now!" often leads to no observable change in Mary's behavior, simply because she often does not know what else to do! Say instead, "Mary, come over to this chair and finish this picture" or the like.

After the crisis, check back with the parties involved a little later and see if all is going well. This can be a brief, informal check. If there seems to be a new problem or any residues such as negative feelings leading to new, but nevertheless, inappropriate behavior, bring all parties back together with a firm message that "Things do not seem to be working out according to our agreement. We need to talk some more." Then begin again and work through the CLEAR steps until the problem is "CLEARed up!"

The crisis intervention methods proposed in this chapter will have relatively little "life" to them unless two further activities are completed by you, the careful reader. First, you will find it most helpful to read the following case history material. Next, you must also try out these ideas and behaviors! The first such trial can occur as you respond to the situations in the Posttest Questionnaire, which is provided toward the end of the book.

We are sure that many of you are already familiar with these techniques and have found them effective with children to whom you respond or to whom you are responsible. In some cases, however, the techniques described may seem unrealistic or not applicable to the situation in which you find yourself. It has been our experience, however, that they are almost always applicable, in almost any relationship with a caring adult and a child in need. We're not going to ask you to take our word for it. We're going to ask you to join us in an examination of a number of illustrations from practice in which these techniques were useful. These are presented in the case illustrations in chapter 4, but being convinced, as we are, is not enough. You'll have to try these techniques, test them in practice. If you do, we are almost certain that you will share with us the conviction that such attitudes and intervention techniques do work.

This approach in dealing with children is rewarded over and over by being a much more satisfying way of interacting with children, and by freeing the group situation from disruptive incidents (as such crises diminish in frequency over time) so that other more academic and/or more rewarding social events can occur. And this system of reacting to children in certain ways provides positive modeling to them for developing their own desirable problem-solving techniques.

Remember the behavioral steps to be used in crisis intervention by the acronym of CLEAR:

C   Control the situation

L   Listen fully

E   Explore alternatives

A   Agree on a solution

R   Resume normal activities *or*
      Renegotiate the entire solution

As will be seen in the case histories in the following chapter, some of these steps may actually be implemented over a period of several days or even a week or so; in other situations, the process may move more quickly through each of the steps. Indeed, as you, the responsible adult, become more skilled in being a "grown-up" guide, mutually satisfactory resolutions can be obtained more and more quickly by all of the participants in the crisis. Then, truly, are crises CLEARed up!

Chapter 4

CASE HISTORIES, OR . . .
"YES, IT DOES WORK . . ."

In this chapter we will present, in simulated transcript form, the interactions involved in crisis intervention. In the first example, there is a problem between an adult and a child in which a third person (an adult) intervenes. Next, we present a conflict between an adult and a child where there is no third party present. Therefore, the involved adult takes on the responsibility of guiding the problem to resolution. Third, two children have a problem. A third-party adult acts as a guide through the process of problem-solving.

An adult using the methods proposed herein should always remember that at no point in time is the situation irreversible. That is, if negotiations break down on a verbal level, the adult should start at the beginning with C—control of the situation—and patiently work through the entire set of steps. Discerning and experienced child care workers will recognize that it is often quite difficult to allot time enough to work in this fashion. We would respond to this quite justifiable concern with the proposition that you really don't have any other option if you want the children who are your charges to learn "grown-up" behaviors. Also, the amount of time required to accomplish positive results may require that the process, from beginning to end, be spaced out over several days rather than concentrated in two to three hours (as is sometimes the case with very difficult crises).

In the following case histories "what to do" is given in the first column, "how" or the specific words and actions are given in the second column, and "why" or the rationale and comments in the third column. The "when" is implied in the order of the entries in the three column tables.

CASE HISTORY 1: An adult-child problem with a second adult acting as the problem-solving guide. *The Situation:* A crisis intervention staff member is asked to come to the dormitory area of a residential facility for children. Johnny and a staff member on that floor, Ms. Brown, are found in head-on confrontation over the refusal of Johnny to comply with Ms. Brown's directive that he remain on the floor while the other children go swimming this evening. Johnny has an awful cold. Johnny is angry, disappointed, and verbally threatening to hit Ms. Brown.

WHAT	HOW	WHY
I. Control the Situation		
A. Enter the problem situation as objectively as possible, initially holding back on making assumptions as to who's at fault and/or on immediately siding with either person. Simply acknowledge the situation and the feelings you perceive there.	A. "This is a real battle!" "Things seem our of control here;" "Everyone is really angry!"	A. A brief, nonblaming acknowledgment of the existence of a problem and the existence of disruptive and negative feelings being expressed by the participants.
B. Be firm. Give directives and directions regarding alternative activities, physical locales, etc. to separate the conflicting parties, to give time for emotions to subside and for people to collect them-	B. "Ms. Brown, please sit right here. Johnny, bring me that chair. Mr. Kowen, please take the other children to the lounge now. Now, just no one speak for a little while." (Sit quietly for a little while.)	B. Use a low tone of voice, but with strength and firmness. Body posture should be restrained and sure. Body movements slow, deliberate, and sure. Be alert for flying objects, blows from an angry child, need

WHAT	HOW	WHY
selves. Move physically between the two opposing parties, if necessary.		for any physical restraints. Be sure when you give directives that you do so in a form that clearly communicates the lack of choice, if none is intended. Thus, Ms. Brown is not *asked* if she "would *like* to sit down," but rather is firmly but gently told to do so. Questions are for information, directives are non-choice commands. Do not confuse them in the crisis situation.
II. *Listen Fully* Find out what has happened *in the present situation only*, when each party can tell you.	"Johnny, tell me what happened . . ."; "Ms. Brown, tell me what happened . . ." (Listen with total attention to each person). "Johnny, do you understand what Ms. Brown just said?"; "Ms. Brown, what did Johnny say?"	Allow neither party to interrupt before the other finishes speaking. Sometimes this is difficult because when each party hears the perceptions of the other, they are often at great variance from their own interpretation of what happened. It is essential to the negotiation process that each of the involved

WHAT	HOW	WHY
		parties understand that they each view what happened very differently. Asking the people at odds with each other to verbalize what the other one said is the first step toward mutual understanding.
III. *Explore Alternatives* A. Look for other possible choices for each participant's behavior. It may be somewhere along this line that one or all of the parties may spontaneously offer an apology to the other parties; or may do so when suggested by the crisis intervention person. Reparation may also be undertaken at this stage.	A. "Johnny, what could you have done just now instead of cursing and throwing the chair when you were disappointed about not going swimming?" "Ms. Brown, what are some other ways in which you could have told Johnny that you believe that it was not good for him to go swimming this evening?" "Ms. Brown, I'm really sorry I yelled." Or, Ms. Brown on the other hand may say, "Johnny, I really didn't understand how badly you wanted to go swimming. I'm sorry."	A. This explanation allows both parties to learn from it, to shift from physical to more objective verbal means of handling the difference. Note here that the adult involved in the conflict should be *as* ready, if not more so, to apologize to the child, as to expect that the child *always* be the one to make this overture.

WHAT	HOW	WHY
B. Look for alternative behaviors to the participants' behaviors in future, similar situations.		
(1) Suggest or help the parties generate the next immediate appropriate activities for each.	(1) "It seems that the next thing for all of us to do is to assist the other children in getting ready for the swimming and to decide on what will be done for Johnny."	(1) These are simple statements, simple possibilities with no advice-giving, no solution-giving, no commands or demands by any of the persons involved.
(2) List or otherwise enumerate the long-range behavioral alternatives of each person in similar situations.	(2) "It seems that Johnny is suggesting that when he finds himself upset in the future, he may simply say so—as a fact—rather than throwing a chair or cursing." "Ms. Brown is saying that she can attend to Johnny's concern about being left out of this group's activities."	(2) The clear implication here is that the parties involved are capable, with some assistance, of coming up with better and more appropriate immediate and long-range future behaviors.
IV. *Agreement on Plan of Action*		
A. Decide on next immediate steps to be taken. Get an agreement	A. "Because Johnny cannot both go swimming and not go swimming,	A. Still, no blame-placing, no "punishment" to be meted out,

WHAT	HOW	WHY
about the actions each will take right now and an agreement about the actions that might be important in a longer-range solution.	what are we going to do?" (Allow time for both parties to consider all listed alternatives.) "O.K., is it agreeable for Johnny to get in a warm tub now and then go on to bed for the night and for Ms. Brown to check with the nurse in the morning to see if Johnny can go swimming tomorrow night?" Be sure both parties agree on and can restate the agreement.	rather a problem to be explored and resolved to all parties' satisfaction.
B. If necessary, set up times for follow-up discussions with each party separately or with both parties together to work out the new long-range solution.	B. "What we really need to work on is ways of handling this kind of thing when you have a difference again. When can we talk about this more?" (Set a time.)	B. Times set for later conference should be fairly soon. The appointment should be scrupulously kept by all parties.
C. Stay involved until the immediate solution is implemented by both parties. Recognize and reward cool tempers, reconciliatory efforts, compliance with agreement.	C. "O.K., Johnny, do you need any help in getting your bath started?" (If so, see that he gets it.) "Ms. Brown, will you be sure to check with the nurse the first thing in	C. Do not rush this or any other step in crisis intervention work. It takes time for all parties to cool down, to talk it over, and to move and act more appropriately. Notice

WHAT	HOW	WHY
	the morning?" (This is a wait-and-see time. Do not leave any unextinguished sparks.) "Everybody O.K. for the night?" "All of us are tired now but you really made a lot of progress with each other tonight. I'll see you _____ (time set in step B above)."	at this point, the intervening adult is asking questions, rather than giving commands. Control is thus being gradually returned to the parties involved. If this control is accepted, the "sparks," as well as the "fire," are likely out.
D. Keep those appointments. Work through the problem as a consultant, leaving the responsibility for solution and implementation with the parties involved insofar as possible.	D. "Ms. Brown, how can you deal with Johnny's disappointment when he cannot do something that he wants to do?" (Discuss alternatives.) "Johnny, how can you let someone know that you are disappointed and angry without cursing and throwing things?" (Discuss alternatives.) To both: "Now, we've agreed that when Johnny is angry, he will go punch on the punching bag; and Ms. Brown will try and find some other activity to do when Johnny can't do exactly what he wants to do for some reason."	D. These appointments and discussions should be serious problem-solving sessions held in private and repeated until agreements (and even contracts, if necessary) can be made between the two parties.

WHAT	HOW	WHY
E. Check back in a week or so to see how the new ways are working.	E. "Johnny, are you hitting that punching bag? Have you been angry enough to do that?" "Ms. Brown, are you having any problems in coming up with alternative activities for Johnny when you need them?"	E. Checking back like this shows that you do care and that you do want things to go well between them. Checking back also lets both parties know again that you view the agreements made between them as serious commitments. Making a note in your personal calendar or appointment book will help remind you of this important responsibility.

V. Resume Normal Activities

WHAT	HOW	WHY
A. Resume normal activities if agreement is working. If agreement is working, *exit*. Stay out of it, turn loose completely. Wait until you are called on for aid again.	A. "Oh, that's great. Johnny, it takes a lot of self-control to remember to hit that bag. Ms. Brown, you're really in tune with Johnny now. 'See you'." (Leave.)	A. Don't keep working on now nonexistent problems. Turn loose. People "grow up" when given responsibility they can handle.
OR		
B. Renegotiate to a different agreement. If the original agreement is	B. "Oh, let's get straight on this. We still have a problem and we	B. Yes, this *is* hard work. Yes, sometimes problem-solving has to

WHAT	HOW	WHY
not working, go back to Step I (Control) and work through all the steps above again to another solution.	need to sit down and work it out." (Then, do so!)	be done again and again. But, yes, the results are worth it!

NOTE: Depending on the requirements of the child's educational program plan, the incident log, the communication system of the agency, the teaching potential believed to be inherent in the crisis situation and solution, and so on, the adult who served as the crisis intervention agent may make a brief report of these transactions. An example from the above incident might be: "Problem was Johnny's disappointment re: Ms. Brown's not allowing him to swim when he had a cold. Johnny's resultant anger took the form of cursing and threats of physical aggression. The parties agreed (1) Johnny would hit the bag when he is angry; (2) Ms. Brown will try to redirect Johnny to another enjoyable activity when he is disappointed and pay more attention to his sensitivity about being 'left out.' Agreement is working (Date, name of person making report)." Such brief notes tell other staff persons about the agreement and serves also as a memory aid if the exact conditions that were agreed on need to be retrieved by any of the participants in the crisis situation. Obviously, we think such notes are valuable and recommend that some system for them be developed. After many entries have accumulated, the system will serve as a great way to retrieve effective methods of crisis management, serve as a realistic introduction for new employees, and show the administrators how hard we all work!

CASE HISTORY 2: An adult-child problem with the first beginning the meal, but then dawdles and seems involved adult acting as a problem-solving guide. *The* only to push the remaining foods about (a considerable *Situation:* Margaret, age 8, is taken by her parents to a amount of food remains). Her mother quietly requests local cafeteria for supper. She is allowed to select her that Margaret complete her meal. Margaret laughs and own food from the attractive array. She eats well when smirks, "You can't make me!"

WHAT	HOW	WHY
I. *Control the Situation*		
A. Separate the fuel and the fire here for adequate control.	A. "Margaret, come with me." (Physically assist the child as needed. Accompany the child to the ladies' room, to the auto outside, or to any other area away from the rest of the family and the other diners.)	A. Audiences are not helpful during conflict resolution sessions! Furthermore, other persons have a right to eat their meal with their usual composure—a composure which might be threatened by overhearing a serious problem-solving situation.
B. Acknowledge the problem from your perspective.	B. Mother: "We seem to have a problem, Margaret. I am upset when I see food wasted and when you speak to me in such a manner. How do you feel?"	B. The adult states her own concerns, using personal pronouns and feelings (*I* am *upset*) and invites child to respond.

WHAT	HOW	WHY
II. *Listen Fully*		
	Margaret: "You're always on to me to eat. I ate enough! And, I'm not going to eat anymore!"	
	Adult: "You feel resentful when I urge you to eat!"	The adult shifts gears into active listening to facilitate communication and understanding.
	Margaret: "Yeh. and I'm big enough to eat without you *talking* to me about it!"	Listen for the "Yeh." It signals an accurate reflection of the feelings and thoughts expressed.
	Adult: "You're unhappy that I don't treat you more like a big girl."	
	Margaret: "Yeh, I don't need to be told what to eat or how much to eat anymore!"	

WHAT	HOW	WHY
	Adult: "You feel you can handle this all by yourself. O.K."	The adult now understands child's position; half the battle is won because Margaret is sure the adult knows why she is behaving the way she is. The groundwork is also laid for Margaret now to listen to the adult in a reciprocal process.
	Margaret: "Yes."	
	Adult: "But I still feel unhappy when we pay for food, as high as it is now, and it's just left on a plate. What can we do?"	Adult reiterates her own position. Timing is important here. As the child, Margaret's position is explored *first*, allowing her to direct her energies to understanding the adult after first being understood.
III. *Explore Alternatives*	Margaret: "I guess I could cut down on how much I put on my tray—or I could take leftovers home for Ralph in a . . . a . . ."	Child suggests three alternatives while the adult waits to hear all three.
	Mother: "Doggie bag?"	

WHAT	HOW	WHY
	Margaret: "Yeh. And maybe Daddy will eat the rest of my rice and gravy.	
	Mother: "Cutting down on how much food you select is O.K. with me. But the vet said not to feed Ralph table foods. And it's not O.K. with me for Daddy to eat the foods you leave.	Mother evaluates each alternative, giving feedback regarding their acceptability.
	Margaret: "Well, if you just won't say anymore about it, I won't get so much the next time."	
	Mother: "O.K., fine."	
	Margaret: "O.K., let's go."	

WHAT	HOW	WHY
I. *Control the Situation*		
A. Remain separated from the problem site until everything is worked through.	A. Mother: "Nope. Not yet. I'm still upset about the tone of voice you used when you said, 'You can't make me'!"	A. This is an example of renegotiating back through the CLEAR steps again, this time dealing with the adult's remaining concern.
	Margaret: "I'm sorry. *I won't do it again!*" (with sign of dramatic resignation).	
B. Acknowledge the remaining problems.	B. Mother: "Just that statement in that manner is not good enough.	B. For effective resolution all major issues need to be dealt with to the satisfaction of the parties involved.
	Margaret, am I right to think you feel defiant at times . . . you feel ready to test me to see if I can and will back up requests I make of you with *force*, if necessary?"	The adult has listened and chosen not to accept a too-quick, questionably sincere "capitulation" on the part of the child. The adult here seems to think a "spark" remains between them and thus attempts to figure out, with the child's help, what it is and then resolve it.

WHAT	HOW	WHY
II. *Listen Fully*	Margaret: "Oh, I just said that. I don't think you'd beat me or anything!"	
	Mother: "You just feel resentful and expressed it to me in that way?"	
III. *Explore Alternatives*	Margaret: "Yeh, I should have waited 'til we were home or somewhere alone. 'Sorry I said . . . that other thing."	Apologies sometimes come spontaneously.
	Mother: "O.K., good. Next time you're feeling bugged by me—you will do what?"	Mother *allows* expression of negative feelings of the child yet continues to request alternatives.
	Margaret: "I'll tell you I want to tell you something in my room	Be ready. Children often will bargain!

WHAT	HOW	WHY
	and then I will talk—but you mustn't get mad at me!"	
IV. *Agree on Plan of Action*	Mother: "O.K., I think I will not get nearly so upset if we talk in private rather than in a public place."	Agreement by adult is specified so that child understands what is being agreed to. An "O.K." by itself is often confusing and can lead to further misunderstanding.
	Margaret: "O.K." (Hugs mother).	Acknowledgment of resolution is often a pleasant physical demonstration that is reassuring to both parties.
V. *Resume Normal Activities*	Mother (returning hug): "Now, let's go back to Daddy and the boys. We may get home in time for Daddy to go to his meeting on time yet."	Hugging, shaking hands, etc. can be powerful forms of emotional commitment. Fostering them is an important part of the conflict resolution process because people who

WHAT	HOW	WHY
		can tolerate (and even *enjoy*) physical contact are seldom at odds with the resolution of the conflict. The implication here is that both parents value this method; for example, the father may have been late to, or missed his scheduled after-dinner evening meeting if Mother and Margaret's conflict resolution session had been a lengthy one.

NOTE: In conflict resolution of family problems a record may not be necessary. In a group home, however, it may be very desirable for the reasons mentioned in the first case history in this chapter. If such is the case, the adult might note: "Margaret left much food at meal and spoke in unpleasant manner. Agreed Margaret not take so much food, I not treat her "like baby." Margaret will express negative feelings toward me at home in private, rather than in public place."

CASE HISTORY 3: A child-child problem with attending adult acting as problem-solving guide. *The Situation:* Susan and Bobby are seated at worktable during art time at kindergarten. Both reach for the crayons (only one box is visible) at about the same time. Susan picks up the crayon box first. With quickly rising voices, we hear, "Mine!" "Let go!" "No!" "I want 'em!" "I need them!" "Teacher, make Bobby let go of these crayons!" (Both shriek.) "He hit me!" (Chair overturns.) Teacher comes over.

WHAT	HOW	WHY
I. *Control the Situation*		
A. Separate the contestants.	A. "Susan, sit here. Bobby, give me the crayons. Pick up that chair. O.K." (adult pointing). "Bobby, now sit here." (Pause.)	A. If Bobby is allowed to hold crayons *during* the conflict-resolution, Susan will probably perceive that Bobby has "won," and so will see no point to further negotiation.
B. Recognize that a problem exists.	B. "We have a problem."	
II. *Listen Fully*	"I want each of you to tell me what you remember happened. Susan, you stop crying while Bobby talks to us, then you will tell me what you remember. Now, Bobby, what do you remember?" (Listen all the	Volume low, calm. Orderly approach helps children to cool down. This exchange should also proceed at a fairly slow pace to assist in the "cooling down" process. Having children "tell their side

64

WHAT	HOW	WHY
	way.) "And you feel that you were going to lose the crayons?" When Bobby has finished: "Now Susan. You tell me what you remember." (Listen. Do not allow Bobby to interrupt.) "O.K. Good. It sounds to me like both of you wanted the crayons at the same time and were afraid that you wouldn't get them!"	communicates that there is no one objective truth but that we have different perceptions because we usually view events from different vantage points.
III. *Explore Alternatives*	"Susan, if Bobby wanted crayons and you had them, how could he let you know that?" (No answer.) "Bobby, what could you have done instead of hitting Susan?" (Both children silent.) "Well, as I see it, Bobby could have either not gotten crayons at all; or he could have asked Susan for part of the crayons; or Bobby could have asked me for another pack of	With very young children, the adult often has to help generate alternatives. In this light, it is also helpful to judge mentally retarded and/or emotionally disturbed chil-

WHAT	HOW	WHY
	crayons. Another idea is that maybe Susan could use the crayons today and then Bobby could use them tomorrow." (Children tell why each alternative O.K. or not O.K. with them.)	dren as being less capable of generating useful alternatives, thus needing more help from the adult during this phase of crisis resolution.
IV. *Agree on Plan of Action*	"Well, it seems that it is O.K. with both of you for Bobby to ask me for another pack of crayons. Is that right?" (Children nod.) "O.K., let's see what we do next. Bobby you have already picked up the chair."	Check out the agreement to make sure no "sparks" are left. Reparation already made.
A. Next immediate things for children to do.	A. "Susan, will you go up to my table and get another box of crayons? Bobby, what colors were you going to use?" (Susan returns with crayons.) "Fine. Thank you, Susan. Now, Susan, give that pack to	A. This exchange nonverbally (as far as the children are concerned) reinforces the *concept of sharing*, by having one child transmit materials to the other.

WHAT	HOW	WHY
	Bobby. Here are the ones that you had." (Give the original package to Susan.)	
B. Behavior in future similar situations.	B. "Bobby, what will you do the next time Susan is holding something you want?" (If he replies that he will ask the teacher for another item, or that he will ask Susan to share, accept and praise this answer.)	B. Care must be taken here to speak in a nonpunitive, matter-of-fact voice.
	"Susan, what if Bobby wants something you are holding—tomorrow, say—what would you do?" (No answer.)	*Both* children have responsibility in the situation.
	"O.K. Susan, hold this book. Bobby pretend you want that book and try to get it." (Bobby stands, grins, and reaches out to take book.) Susan cries, "No, go get another one—teacher, Bobby wants to take my book!" (Teacher steps between the children.) "Susan, we	Role-play "What if . . ." with children who are not very adept at hypothesizing and verbalization of their own probable future behavior.

WHAT	HOW	WHY
	agreed that you would offer to share with Bobby or else remind him to ask me for another book. What would you say?"	
	Susan: "No, not now. But you can see it when I'm finished."	
	Bobby: "Yeh, I guess so."	
	Teacher: "O.K., let's do that again." (Redo this scene.) "Good, now you know a better way to get what you want, Bobby. And Susan, you know more about sharing!"	Rehearsal for future problem situations is a very effective teaching tool.
V. *Resume Normal Activities*		
	"That's fine." "Bobby, when you finish your drawing, go to the story table and pick out a book. Susan, do you still want to cut out the paper doilies to glue on top of your drawing?"	Always assume that the parties in crisis *can* and *will* resume appropriate behavior.

NOTE: If note needed for records, it might read: "March 19. Susan Brady to ask teacher for duplicate material in future. This was role-played. Both and Bobby Jackson each wanted some crayons at same time. Bobby hit returned to usual activities. (Name of adult.) Susan. Susan cried. Agreed to share by alternate use of some materials or

In each of three preceding case histories, the person responsible for guiding the problem-solving process demonstrated his commitment to the *values* cited in chapter 1. To review, the adult believed in recognizing the human dignity of the parties in the conflict (as shown by hearing them out and so on) as being more important than quick reestablishment of adult domination in the situation by issuing directives, commands, or by use of punishment. Each of the adults also believed that taking time to teach problem-solving skills was as important as bedtime, eating, or art work. Further, in neither situation above did the attending adult *need* to use power or to force *his* solution on others just so he could feel "important," feel "like the boss," or feel "like a winner" at the expense of the children. Finally, all of the adults viewed the children involved as socially unskilled, rather than as "bad." Thus, the adult's efforts were extended toward teaching new behaviors to the child rather than to "punishing" the child.

Chapter 5

GENERALITY, OR . . .
"THIS WILL ALSO WORK WITH . . ."

In this chapter we indicate how the methods discussed can be used in other relationships, in addition to the adult-child dyad, and then follow up by inviting you to respond to the several new situations given in questionnaire form, for broadening your new skills.

What is there about these methods that would argue against their use in *any* relationship? Nothing! Nothing at all!

The exact words exchanged between the parties in a relationship would differ according to the age, sex, race, and ability level of each participant involved. Similarly, the *rate of movement* of the parties through the CLEAR steps when resolving a conflict would also vary, depending on the previously cited variables and on the amount of past experience each party has had in using the methods.

The list of adult-child situations is virtually endless, and you can easily extrapolate these methods to any adult-child interaction in which you may be involved as parent, teacher, child care worker, and as trainer of other child care workers, parents, teachers, and so on.

There are also many relationships that, while they are not between adult and child in the sense of disparate chronological ages of the parties, still share the commonality of being between "caretaker and client," between "trainer and trainee," or between "supervisor and worker." Sometimes, two adults enter into a "helper and helpee" relationship by virtue of one needing the medical or psychological expertise of the other, as in a "doctor-patient" relationship. The attitudinal and behavioral suggestions in this book are particularly important in such cases.

Power tactics at such times reinforce the legitimate dependency needs of the patient, a client, to the point of infantilizing her and thereby artificially extending her recuperation period. As can be anticipated, adults who are treated with power tactics when they are patients in medical facilities often experience incredible resentment and anger at such psychological humiliations—in addition to all necessary physical indignities—and often express hostility via passive-aggressive or overtly uncooperative behaviors. Such expressions drain energies better utilized in the recovery process.

At this point, generalization from adult-child interactions can be made to adult-adult relationships. Between friend and friend, between doctor and patient, between wife and husband, between adult business partners, between two professional colleagues—can you imagine use of these attitudes and methods? Perhaps only a slightly different emphasis is needed in the prevention tactics—only a recognition that CLEAR solutions develop and enhance the positive relationship between the parties. Another shift may be necessary: In an adult-adult relationship, neither party is presumably responsible for "educating," "guiding," "rearing," "teaching," "training," "monitoring," or "directing" the other—as is the case in adult-child relationships. In the adult-adult dyad, each is responsible for her own behavior and both are responsible for the quality of the relationship. As the relationship is simply the sum total of all of the transactions between the two participants, the quality of the relationship may be interpreted to mean the proportion of total transactions that are concluded to the benefit and satisfaction of both parties. Using CLEAR techniques causes that proportion of successes to grow!

And finally, these attitudes and methods are fully as useful in group interactions and efforts. Admittedly, all of the members of the group have to be reasonable and at least willing to *try* to reach solutions to conflicts within the group by using these methods. It has been our experience that when an adult group member is motivated to be cooperative, the actual procedural steps in conflict resolution can be understood in a matter of a few minutes. When a group member is not desirous of reaching an agreement, then all the explanations in the world are to no avail! At these times, it is suggested that you quietly ask such a person: "Shall we simply agree to disagree and to continue to do things—each in our own way, or, would you like to continue to discuss this matter until we reach a solution which is acceptable to us both?" This question, and its answer, can often get the process moving again.

The knowledge and use of orderly, verbal problem prevention and problem resolution skills increases the probability that human interactions will be ethically responsible and personally rewarding!

CLEAR METHODS IN OTHER SITUATIONS

Here, we would like to use the following situations for practice to discern your understandings of how the CLEAR procedures can be useful in conflict situation in settings other than the adult-child relationships. Read each situation carefully and record your response in the space provided. If you have problems in deciding what to do, refer back to the section on CLEAR procedures and see if you can extrapolate appropriate responses. Here are a few hints. Remember, there are no absolutely correct answers but rather ones that include, first, gaining a bit of time to solve the problem (control the situation); second, finding out and discussing what you and the other person involved are thinking and feeling (listening fully); third, looking for mutually acceptable ways to resolve the impass (exploring alternatives); fourth, picking one of the mutually acceptable ways (agreeing on a plan); and finally, going on about your business (resuming normal activities).

(1) Janice looks up from the department store sales ad in the newspaper with the comment, "I'm going to run over to Davidson's at lunch and take advantage of this sale!" Emily responds, "But I was supposed to meet Paul for lunch today at noon—and one of us must stay here to cover the phone!" You, as Janice, then propose: _____

_____

_____

_____

_____

(2) You sit, with increasing resentment, in the waiting room of Dr. Franklin. Your appointment time came and passed 35 minutes ago. You need medical attention, but your first-grader will be waiting for you to pick her up at school in 30 minutes—a drive of at least 10 minutes. You respond to the situation by: _____

_____

_____

_____

_____

(3) Dirty dishes greet your gaze as you finish dinner. Your roommate says, "That was a terrific dinner, Georgia," as she moves from the table to the easy chair and her newspaper. You, as Georgia, respond: _____

_____

_____

_____

_____

(4) A friend, Ed, tells you in a confidential tone, "Bill, if Martha asks, be sure to tell her that you and I were working late together at the office last Tuesday night—you will, won't you, old buddy?" Ed's wink and grin as he moves away leaves you momentarily without a reply. You, as Bill, decide to: _____

_____

_____

_____

_____

(5) As a new (female) faculty member, you notice that the male principal of your secondary school repeatedly assigns you the task of taking notes

at faculty meetings. This chore prevents you from entering into the discussions as you desire to do. Besides, to rewrite and to type up these minutes takes at least two hours of your time after each such meeting. You decide to: _____

_____

_____

_____

_____

Chapter 6

TECHNICAL REFERENCES, OR . . .
"OTHER FOLKS THINK SO, TOO . . ."

Throughout this book we have attempted to keep the references to technical material at an absolute minimum. However, many of the ideas and concepts in this small book come from previous writers and theoreticians in the areas of interpersonal skills, social skills training, social learning theory, rational emotive therapy, parent effectiveness training, behavior therapy, and strict operant conditioning procedures. In order to provide the reader with references for further study and reading in these areas, this chapter will detail some of the specific writings and programs of other authors and researchers.

Primary to our references are the works of Carkhuff (1973), Gordon (1970) and Ivey and Gluckstern (1974). These several authors present material essential to the helping process. They outline in clear and concise programmatic steps the individual and component skills for reflective listening, client-centered therapy, and effective interpersonal communications. The basic premise of these authors is that by learning to communicate effectively to other people that we understand what they are saying, we can begin to negotiate on a common basis. Without these skills, most human interactions are doomed to misunderstanding, confusion, and distortion. This is true because the parties are not working from the same frame of reference in exchanging information and other messages. The communication skills contained in these books lay the groundwork for effective work with children *and* adults in the verbal communication mode. We also strongly endorse Smith (1975) as a basic work describing personal rights, assertive responding, and dealing with difficult adult interpersonal interactions.

It is our hearty recommendation that these materials be read, studied, and actively practiced in order that the reader will develop the skills to understand accurately and to communicate that understanding to the individuals with whom he interacts. These works include videotape demonstrations and activities to ensure that the skills being presented are incorporated into the adult's repertoire of communication skills. Gordon's emphasis on techniques of conflict resolution begins with techniques useful when there is a conflict of *needs* and proceeds to teach another set of skills to use when there is a conflict of *values*. This distinction makes his work highly valuable as a resource and background material for people working with children and others in crisis intervention situations.

Turning to research-based materials, we recommend that crisis workers become familiar with the literature in the area of social skills training with children, such as Combs and Slaby (1977). In addition to a review of the literature in the area of social interaction training with children, these authors point out such important areas as the possible negative effects of a misapplication of social interaction training with children (such as reinforcing inappropriate behavior). This has to do with the timing of the verbal and social reinforcers, the influence of peers in developing social and interpersonal competencies, the use of modeling for the development of appropriate (and unfortunately, inappropriate) interactions, and the research on role-playing, coaching, and active problem solving.

Of undisputed importance is the work of Ayllon and Rosenbaum (1977). These authors present research data which concludes that the *socially disruptive* behaviors of children can be effectively eliminated by reinforcing appropriate *academic* achievements! These reseachers cleverly demonstrate that reinforcing behaviors that compete with disruptive behaviors (i.e., academically appropriate responses) leads to the virtual elimination of inappropriate social behavior. This research has had a great impact on social learning and operant conditioning theories. It is a hallmark example of our premise that working on developing appropriate social and academic skills is the most effective way to prevent crisis behaviors from occurring. This article also contains many useful references for some of the work that has been done in eliminating discipline problems through operant conditioning procedures.

As we have pointed out in previous sections, many of the problems associated with crises in child treatment settings occur because adults hold inappropriate attitudes toward children—attitudes that are incompatible with effective conflict resolution techniques. In this area, we recommend that child care workers and parents become familiar with the work of Hauck (1977) and Dreikers, Gould, and Corsini (1974). These two references detail the interaction and meaning of interactional patterns between parents and children. Dreikers et al. focus on what behaviors children display in order to meet their needs, whereas Hauck examines common errors and irrational attitudes of parents in dealing with their children. Many useful ideas, examples, and interactional patterns are presented therein that meld well with the material in this book.

Consistent with Hauck, and in line with the discussion of self-help and self-regulatory behaviors in this book, is the work of Meichenbaum (1977). Meichenbaum explains the self-instructional training paradigm and the application of cognitive factors. This discussion provides additional useful dialogue related to the crisis resolution stages presented in this book. Meichenbaum clearly presents evidence that what children tell themselves in the form of scary, irrational, or faulty thinking adversely affects their ability to solve problems and to cope effectively with crisis situations.

By becoming familiar with both the irrational beliefs and the faulty thinking that can occur in children (and adults), child care workers can effectively restructure the child's perceptions of the situation. When the child's view of the problem is changed, the usual emotions of outrage, fear, and aggression are then circumvented. Irrational belief systems are also held by therapists and others responsible for positive change occurring among children. For more understanding in this area, we recommend Janzen and Myers (in press). Specifically, this paper deals with the negative attitudes and beliefs that many helpers have that *directly* contribute to the problems of those individuals they are trying to help.

We have mentioned using the natural environment as a "restitution bearer" for any display of inappropriate behaviors by the child. Very interesting information in this area has been presented by Foxx and Azrin (1972) and by Glasser (1965). These authors inform us that practice of appropriate social skills very soon after rule infractions occur is a very effective method for insuring that the child involved develops a socially appropriate behavior to replace the ineffective behavior just displayed. Glasser takes a more philosophical approach whereas Foxx and Azrin present the same type of material in a more or less operant conditioning paradigm. Both approaches are useful in providing alternative ways to employ the naturally available environment in teaching coping and problem-solving skills.

Finally, we direct the reader to the works of Kohlberg (1963) regarding the sequence involved in the development of moral codes in children and adults. Kohlberg presents stages of moral development beginning with behavior being determined by external and physical consequences (rewards and punishments dispensed by others), through intermediate stages, and finally up through the enlightened altruism of highly evolved adult behaviors. Kohlberg's work is helpful in determining the level of development of a given child, so that the adult can begin prevention and intervention work with that child at the pragmatically optimal point. This means that if such intervention is initiated at the proper level, the child will immediately understand and be able to operate on the premises and directives being provided by the adult.

Although the above list is by no means complete, the foregoing provides a beginning set of references for further exploration of the skills proposed in this book. We hope that each person working intimately with children will become familiar with these works in order to develop a well-rounded perspective on dealing with children in problem situations.

We respectfully suggest that the quickest and surest way any child care worker can increase the pleasure and gratification gleaned from work with children is to *become expert* in that work! We, as professionals, are now far beyond any reason for reacting to our young charges merely out of "good intentions," from the "that's-the-way-my-mother-did-it" rationale, or from our compassionate hunches. We now have specific *skills*, instead! And incorporating these skills in problem prevention and crisis intervention into our everyday work with children leads to a sense of purpose, professionalism, and justified pride!

POSTTEST QUESTIONNAIRE

Using your new skills and understanding of crisis prevention and intervention techniques, read each of the following situations carefully and then record your response in the space provided.

(1) Carrie ignores questions directed to her by her visiting grandparents, slams her fork down into her plate, pushes away from the table, and exits the dining room with a mock and dramatic, "Excuse me, please!" You, as her parent, respond by: _____

_____

_____

_____

_____

(2) All afternoon on a beautiful spring day, Ned has sat, doing nothing, in the big chair in the den. You have suggested recreational activities and some household jobs that could use his attention. Still he just sits and periodically emits a deep, audible sigh. You hand him the new *Children's Life* magazine, which has just come in the mail. He throws it across the room, stating in gruff tones, "Leave me alone!" You respond: _____

_____

_____

_____

_____

(3) Your baking and TV watching are interrupted by sounds from the backyard. You go out to see sand flying, sandpails being hurled, and a general melee underway. You respond by: _____

_____

_____

_____

_____

(4) "I want to sit in the front seat!" "No, you don't, it's my turn, you dummy!" "You always get to sit in the front!" "No, I don't!" "Yes, you do!" "Momma, can't I sit with you?" This is the "conversation" as you embark on an errand by car. You respond by: _____

_____

_____

_____

_____

(5) "Janie's got a boyfriend! Janie's got a boyfriend!" "No, I don't! You stop that!" "Janie's an old maid!" "Janie ain't got NO friends!" You're the Girl Scout leader whose camping trip has suddenly taken an unpleasant turn. You respond by: _____

_____

_____

_____

_____

(6) In a rush to go up to the screen to point out the key blocking position for the play, Luke jars the table holding the slide projector. The projector crashes to the floor, spilling out the slides, and more disturbingly, cracking the glass lens of the projector! You are the coach of this

junior high football team which is having a "skull session." You
handle this problem by: _____

_____

_____

_____

_____

(7) On the faces of all the persons shown in an expensive book of art
reproductions, you see that ink (!!) moustaches, scars, and other dis-
figurements have been drawn! One of your students must have done
this! Your beautiful and treasured book is ruined. You respond by: __

_____

_____

_____

_____

(8) "May I go to the bathroom?" "Let me pass those out," "I know, I
know, let me answer," "I'm through, teacher, I'm through," "Is that
right? That's right, isn't it, teacher?" and on and on—such are the
hundreds of messages received from young Mark each day. You and
other teachers have discussed many times these "attention-getting"
behaviors of Mark. You decide to: _____

_____

_____

_____

_____

(9) You've silently nicknamed Harry, "The Hopper," because each day,
he is "impossible" after a couple of hours of conformity and earnest
involvement in the classroom tasks. You realize that if you allow him

alternative activities, a change of pace, or the option of attending only a part day of school, other students may press for similar concessions. You are the assistant principal who "gets to" make a decision about how best to handle The Hopper. You decide to: _____

_____

_____

_____

_____

(10) Fellow teachers have suggested having Jim (1) write "I will not steal" 500 times; (2) remain home from school on suspension for two weeks; (3) lose recess and all special field trips for a month or the like as consequences for his having taken Joan's phonograph records. You have the final say so about what happens to "sticky-fingered" Jim. Your decision: _____

_____

_____

_____

_____

For suggested answers and explanations to both the pretest and the posttest items, turn to the Appendix.

REFERENCES

Ayllon, T., & Rosenbaum, M. S. The behavioral treatment of disruption and hyperactivity in school settings. In B. B. Lahey & A. E. Kazdin (Eds.) *Advances in clinical child psychology.* New York: Plenum Press, 1977.

Carkhuff, R. R. *The art of helping: A guide for developing helping skills for parents, teachers, and counselors.* Amherst, Mass.: Human Resource Development Press, 1973.

Combs, M. C., & Slaby, D. A. Social skills training with children. In B. B. Lahey & A. D. Kazdin (Eds.) *Advances in clinical child psychology.* New York: Plenum Press, 1977.

Dreikers, R., Gould, S., & Corsini, R. J. *Family council: The Dreikers technique for putting an end to war between parents and children (and children and children).* Chicago: Henry Regnery, 1974.

Foxx, R., & Azrin, N. Restitution: A method of eliminating aggressive-disruptive behavior of retarded and brain-damaged patients. *Behaviour Research and Therapy,* 1972, *10,* 15-27.

Glasser, W. *Reality therapy.* New York: Harper & Row, 1965.

Gordon, T. *Parent effectiveness training.* New York: Peter H. Wyden, Inc., 1970.

Hauck, P. A. Irrational parenting styles. In H. Ellis & R. Grieger (Eds.) *Handbook of rational-emotive therapy.* New York: Springer Publishing Co., 1977.

Ivey, A. E., & Gluckstern, N. B. *Basic attending skills: An introduction to micro-counseling and helping.* North Amherst, Mass.: Microtraining Associates, 1974.

Janzen, W. B., & Myers, D. V. Assertion for therapists: A professional bill of rights. *Psychotherapy: Theory, research, and practice,* in press.

Kohlberg, L. Moral development and identification. In H. W. Stevenson & J. Kagan (Eds.) *Child psychology, the 62nd yearbook of the National Society for the Study of Education.* Chicago: The National Society for the Study of Education, 1963.

Meichenbaum, D. *Cognitive-behavior modification.* New York: Plenum Press, 1977.

Smith, M. *When I say no, I feel guilty.* New York: Bantam Books, 1975.

APPENDIX: COMMENTS ON
PRETEST AND POSTTEST QUESTIONNAIRES

Situations 1. In both the cases of Carolyn and Carrie, the first step is to realize that the child is upset, probably angry in some way. Remember, anger is *fear*. Thus, the first think step is "What is she afraid of?" The suggested behavioral step in both cases is to go to the child and quietly invite further expression of her upset feelings, perhaps by quietly stating, "You feel upset?" Then listen fully and actively, as the child talks. Then, when you realize the child's position, work through the problem by exploring alternatives (to the described unacceptable behaviors), reaching an agreement on an alternative and its implementation.

Situations 2. The examples of Nelson and Ned illustrate the frequent "explosion" of the too-quiet, withdrawn child when adults attempt to energize or to activate him. These responses occur when (1) the child is preoccupied and troubled; (2) the child is not feeling up to par physically; (3) the child is extremely fatigued; or (4) when the child is engaged in mental problem-solving about some real-life conflict. Your responses should be directed at finding out (1) which of these circumstances may pertain; (2) if your intervention and skillful listening are needed or desired by the child; and (3) if continued space, solitude, and quiet are needed.

Situations 3. In both the classroom and sandpile disturbances the first step is to take control of the situation by issuing firm verbal commands, accompanied by physical intervention, if needed. The next step is to listen fully to each participant's story about the events and feelings leading to the fray. And from there, go on through the CLEAR steps. In both situations, give firm commands about what each child is to do immediately ("Marcia, come to me. Fred, sit down here [as you touch the chair]. Janet, put the eraser on your desk.") rather than issuing any statements about what each should *stop* doing, such as "Now, all of you, stop that right now!"

Situations 4. In both of these situations, the central problem is that of two children wanting the same toy or the same privilege at the same time. Here, a calm statement of that being a problem for all concerned is a good beginning. Then, move quickly into asking the combatants for possible solutions, and so on through the CLEAR problem resolution procedure.

Situations 5. In these cases, taunts and name-calling, coupled with the possibility of pending physical aggression, are the central problems. The learning to be promoted is twofold: (1) words can cause pain in another person; and (2) words can be ignored. The attending adult should also be aware that name-calling is sometimes an ineffectual attempt to express affection (really!) for the person so taunted. A quick conference, in private if possible, should be conducted. The attending adult should work toward expression of, and ownership of, the feelings of both parties, and from there, into generation of alternative behaviors that might be used in the future to express these feelings (whether positive or negative).

Situations 6. In the cases of spilt punch and spilt slides, neither was anything but an accident. Neither had any malintentions nor malice involved. Both are best handled by simple statement of the observed effect (rather than accusative statements): "That punch and ice are all over the floor;" "The slides are spilled"; rather than, "Now, look what a mess you've made!" The new learning for the child is best accomplished by reparation (i.e., cleaning up the mess) and by forgetting the entire incident. Even the broken projector lens should be written off, without any punishment to Luke, as "wear and tear"—as an accident. Some time spent examining how to avoid such accidents in the future (i.e., how to anticipate the consequences of one's behavior) will better ensure improved behavior than pointing out how stupid people can be.

Situations 7. Damage to expensive and prized possessions often triggers anger (fear of being devalued, unimportant) in the attending adult. The principle of reparation should be remembered here. But, here, also, Glasser's prior recommendation regarding "confession" will be relevant, as in neither case does the teacher know who did the damage to the prized objects. The next day, the teacher might impress on his students his feelings about the event, invite the responsible parties to speak to him privately about the matter, and suggest that replacement (reparation) may or may not be possible. In both cases we recommend against the entire group losing a privilege or subsequent treat pending someone's taking the blame for the incident. Punishment of the group as a whole is rarely effective in such cases, as it does not change one of the group member's behavior and always results in pitting child against child along lines of the "culprit" versus the "innocents."

Situations 8. In these situations, review your own beliefs about meeting the needs of demanding children, your position on being "manipulated" versus your perception of yourself as a helper whose actions *should* be designed to meet the needs of children in your charge, and your own values and beliefs regarding "legitimate" dependency relationships. In these situations, try again to ask yourself the three think-step questions: "What am I feeling just now?" (the answer will probably be resentment, irritation, fatigue, or the like); "What does the child want?" (the answer will probably be attention, companionship, reassurance, recognition, or the like); and "Is it bad for him to want attention, company, or reassurance?" (the answer is probably "no"). Then you will likely be in a position to respond with attention, to make a statement to the child that you realize that he wants attention or the like, and then, after *giving* to the child, being free to set some limits on further demands at that particular time.

Situations 9. These cases require reexamination of your belief that "every child should be treated as an individual" and your concurrent belief that all the students in your care must be treated "fairly" (sometimes translated to mean "the same"). We have found it (amazingly) sufficient to explain individual adjustments, changes, and programming for one child to the rest of the group by simply stating "Helen's body works differently from yours and to stay healthy, she needs to eat something between each meal. You do not need to do this." Or, "Harry needs to be here only a part of each day. You need to be here all day." Similar comments are appropriate to parents who may question some facet of individual programming for a certain child. The implication is clearly established that should they themselves (the other students or children) need singular adjustments made in the group activities or routine, such would be possible for them as well.

Situations 10. These cases, and suggested solutions, focus on the *aim* of intervention: behavioral change to more appropriate behavior—or revenge and retaliation? Reparation is a first appropriate step in both situations: hosing down the trees and cleaning up the sodden paper, and returning the stolen records to Joan. Far more effective than arbitrary "punishments" is a session with the "culprits" in which they discuss what happened, what they intended, what they can do in such future situations, and so on. With a bit of thought, reparation can be developed in the form of naturalistic amends (repair, restitution, restoration) of the original infraction, rather than assigned tasks designed only to cause the "culprit" retaliative pain, discomfort, or humiliation.

Now, how did you do? Have your answers on the posttest questionnaire changed from those you gave on the pretest? We'd like to know. Please use the questionnaire on the following page to communicate with us at the addresses given. Remember, it is absolutely amazing how much enjoyment and pleasure you can derive from your interaction with children —when you treat them with caring and with respect!

ABOUT THE AUTHORS

CARMIE THRASHER COCHRANE, Ph.D., is a clinical psychologist who has served as psychological consultant to programs for exceptional children in public schools and to educational/treatment agencies for mentally retarded, physically handicapped, emotionally disturbed, gifted and "normal" children and adults. She has also taught human development courses at the university level. Both her present consulting work and professional writings reflect her conviction that competencies in relationship-building, problem-solving, and coping skills are *teachable*, and that such skills constitute powerful deterrents to the development of "mental health" problems. Dr. Cochrane's interests in creativity and craftsmanship are reflected in a prior publication, a cookbook! In addition, she enjoys designing clothes, writing poetry, painting, and being a wife and mother.

DAVID VOIT MYERS, Ph.D., is presently the senior clinical psychologist, University of Alabama Health Center, and Assistant Professor of Psychology at the same institution. In addition to his work experience as a teacher and assistant principal of an elementary school, Dr. Myers has served as a psychologist in public schools, developmental disabilities centers, medical facilities, community mental health centers, and private practice. His theoretical and practical orientation reflects his conviction that deficits in social skills acquisition and expression are at the root of most behavioral and emotional problems of children and adults. In his spare time Dr. Myers enjoys flying his own plane, cycling, and photography.

QUESTIONNAIRE, OR...
"WHATDAYA THINK ABOUT...?"

(Please use back of this page or attached sheets as needed for your replies.)

(1) With which parts of this book did you agree? Which parts should be explained in future editions?

(2) With which parts of this book did you disagree, and why?

(3) What additional pointers, methods, and so on have you found effective in crisis prevention and intervention?

(4) What additional readings, films, training materials, and the like have you found to be effective in teaching such techniques to others?

(5) Your age ____ Sex____ Position _____

No. of years experience in working with children _____

Other information, including name and address if you wish, about yourself and your interest in this work: _____

_____

_____

_____

_____

Please return questionnaire to:

Carmie Thrasher Cochrane, Ph.D.   OR   David Voit Myers, Ph.D.
2301 Capehart Circle, N.E.   P.O. Box 2968
Atlanta, Georgia 30345   University, Alabama 35486